Paper Structures and Scenery for Model Trains

"Strategies, tips and practical projects to easily and affordably create landscapes, buildings and backgrounds your model train layout."

By Dominic Villari

ISBN: 978-0981494050

Published by Figment Press

Foreword

In our hobby, there are a lot of right answers…the right gauge of wire for a certain application, the right radius curve for a locomotive, the right technique for soldering components together. In model railroad scenery, and paper-based scenery specifically, there are no absolute right answers. Scenery is more like a science experiment or an art project. You're never completely sure of the results until you finish and you're only limited by your own creativity.

CONTENTS

Part 1: Strategies and Techniques

Part 2: Specific Projects

1

Overview of Paper Modeling

Introduction to Paper Modeling

History of Paper Modeling

Model Railroad Applications

Sources for Paper Models

Introduction to Paper Modeling

Paper modeling is one of the fastest growing trends in model railroading today. Traditionally, most structures were built out of styrene plastic or balsa wood. Landscaping elements were mainly composed of foam, lichen and similar elements. Paper was literally relegated to the background, suitable for flat buildings glued against a wall to create some depth.

The building on the left is made from paper. The one on the right is plastic.

Over the last decade, model railroaders have become more and more friendly to the idea of using three-dimensional paper-based models on their layouts. The overall affordability of paper over plastic and wood products has certainly been a great motivator. However, the quality of paper-based modeling products has also improved exponentially in recent years.

In addition to being more affordable, paper scenery products can also be more flexible than their plastic and wood counterparts. Paper is easier to bend, can be mounted to a variety of different materials and provides much more control over the thickness of the model. Paper also tends to come in a greater variety. The higher production costs of plastic limit the range of colors and textures.

Paper models also take advantage of photo-realistic images to provide a more "finished" look almost immediately. In most cases plastic and wood must be painted and weathered before it looks realistic. These factors have helped paper-based models to make the leap off the wall and into the center of the layout.

History of Paper Modeling

I remember spending hours as a kid putting together papers models from books. There was an American 4-4-0 locomotive and matching rolling stock, the main street of a small town, farm scene and even a diorama of a cityscape and harbor. You had to carefully punch each piece out of the book (without ripping the little tabs, of course) and the painstakingly create creases in all the right places. Once you had your creases done you could start inserting tabs to shape each model.

These books were a modern twist on a hobby around for decades. Paper modeling itself has been around almost since the invention of paper in forms such as origami and kirigami. These forms were mainly used to create animals until the 1930's, when wartime production had manufacturers looking for alternatives to metal.

Some of the most famous models were created by Wallis Rigby, who applied paper modeling to the creation of boats, planes and trains. Rigby's creations exploded in popularity during World War II and were published in a variety of books and periodicals. Rigby's creations also provided inspiration for cereal companies like Kellogg's and General Mills.

Also feeling the metal pinch, these manufactures had to come up with paper alternatives for product premiums. In some cases, you would send in box tops to get the model. More clever promotions included models printed directly on the back of the box. In most cases you had to collect several boxes to get the full model or scene.

Skyline was the most famous of the cardstock model producers, creating both O and HO scale kits. They are still sought after by collectors today.

For a short time during the postwar era, paper models shared the shelves with early plastic models. Skyline products and Built-Rite models each produced a full line of paper building kits in both O scale and HO scale. However, they found it difficult to compete with plastic models which were often sturdier, easier to build and offered pre-painted finishes.

In fact, both Skyline and Built-Rite also produced plastic models along with their paper and cardboard kits. Petroleum-based plastics revolutionized the toy industry because they were inexpensive and easier to mold. No one gave much of a look back at paper or cardstock.

Over the years a few companies continued to make paper or cardstock models but the market was limited. It was largely a cottage industry producing model books like the ones I worked on as a kid. This would remain the case for the rest of the twentieth century.

Starting in the early 2000's, three factors began setting the stage for paper and card modeling to become popular again. These include inexpensive ink jet printers, greater availability of thicker paper and resources on the Internet.

Ink jet printers allowed hobbyists to print good-looking models at home and thicker paper allowed for

Built-Rite produced a line of less realistic looking yet economical paper model buildings - often sold in sets.

sturdier and more elaborate models. Once people saw the potential, the Internet provided a forum for people to post patterns and models that other people could download and print at home.

The general craft of paper modeling has become complex relatively quickly, including scale model planes, buildings, ships and even figures. These models can involve literally hundreds of pages to create the completed model. Look through these sites and you'll find structures that could be on a model railroad here and there. However, you may have to examine the model closer to determine scale. At the very least they offer plenty of inspiration.

Prior to the last few years, paper modeling in model railroading has been relegated to two main uses: flat backgrounds and paper-mache applications such as mountains and tunnels. In the early days of toy trains, some manufacturers like Lionel, Marx and American Flyer even sold pre-made paper construction tunnels. The marketplace has also seen a rolled product called "mountain paper."

Today model railroads can choose from a variety of products and patterns to create paper-based structures and the introduction of home-based die cutting machines allows for even greater details and more depth in three-dimensional paper or cardstock structures. Ironically, plastic-based products have become much more expensive due to high tooling costs and the growing scarcity of petroleum.

Model Railroad Applications for Paper Modeling

Paper models have several uses in model railroading of any scale, although they are probably most common in O scale with HO running a distant second. The most common application is backgrounds. Many modelers use flat front buildings, mountains and other elements together with painted walls or posters to create more depth on their layout.

Paper scenery has many uses in model railroading including grass, roads, walls, backgrounds and even full buildings.

Background structures are usually mounted to some type of foam board or balsa wood to raise them out from the rear wall of the layout. They are placed behind track or behind three-dimensional buildings to give the illusion that the towns, cities or industries on the layout continue in the distance.

One early trick modelers used was to cut individual buildings out of rolled model railroad backdrops. Early backdrops were illustrations; today's backdrops are usually printed from panoramic photos on large-scale printers. This is another area where technology has caught up with model railroading requirements.

Retaining walls are another natural fit for paper modeling. Many layouts have inclines, upper tiers, insets or back areas that require some type of constructed wall. Building a retaining wall by notching and painting wood blanks is a long and tedious process that can produce mixed results. Using molded plastic is usually quicker but can be extremely expensive, especially on larger layouts.

As mentioned in the previous section, the use of three-dimensional paper models on train layouts has grown tremendously in the last few years. Paper models can be used for just about any structure on a train layout and several models are available in the marketplace. Urban

In this scene, paper-based buildings are fill in the spaces between and behind these ceramic buildings.

structures are the most popular. As with a retaining wall, multi-story and high-rise buildings can be time consuming and/or expensive to build.

Paper models are a great way to fill in gaps on your layout without spending a lot of money or additional plastic kits. Structures placed deeper or further to the back of the layout or behind other structures don't require as much detail. However, with the proper detailing, paper-based structures can also look as good as plastic or wood structures – worthy of a prominent spot on your layout.

Other uses for paper based models including temporary scenery. A well-detailed or high-rail layout can take quite a bit of time to develop. A small one-foot area can take hours and hours to get the scenery just right. This can leave your layout in an unfinished looking state for months or even years. Paper based modeling is a great way to give your layout a "finished" look in a relatively short amount of time.

You can then go back and replace the paper scenery with more detail later. Friends and family get a better idea of your vision and it's a great way to prototype or test out certain looks without spending a lot of time or money.

Another twist is seasonal scenery. Wouldn't it be great to change the look of your layout three or four times a year? It can be a challenge to decorate shops and houses for July 4th, Halloween and Christmas. The decorations must adhere to the model but can't be permanent. Imagine having four different versions of the same building completely customized for the current season of the year. It's an expensive proposition for plastic, but not for paper models.

One of the most notable aspects of using paper to create models and scenery on train layouts is that paper-based projects are generally very "kid friendly." Paper is less expensive and generally easier to cut and glue. It's also more forgiving and simply to correct problems. For example, you can correct a rip, tear or dent by patching with another small piece of paper. You can also use white glue or glue stick rather than the harsh chemical adhesives and solvents required for plastic models.

Paper-based models and scenery are a great way to involve children, grandchildren, nieces, nephews, etc. in model railroading or model building in general. They are generally quicker and easier to put together and the cleanup is much simpler than plastic materials.

Sources for Paper Models

A well-designed model railroad almost always has elements from many different manufacturers. That's the best way to get the diversity of landscaping and structures that occur in real life. It's likely you'll need to combine products from different manufacturers when developing your layout.

Free Internet Sites

A quick Google search on paper models will produce several sites with free models. Model quality is usually good on these sites but the ease of instructions varies from model to model. You may need to figure out some aspects of the model yourself. For this reason, they're not always the best choice for first time modelers. It's also sometimes hard to find a model in the right scale.

There are also sites that offer free textures such as brick and stone. The main drawback to downloadable textures is that the quality is limited to your printer and you must trim the edges of the sheet. Printing your own textures can also be expensive depending on the cost of your ink cartridges. That said, the free sites are a great way to get inspiration, tips and strategies for paper modeling.

Magazine Blueprints

Most of the major model railroading magazines regularly feature structure blueprints. These blueprints are usually scaled down to fit on the pages of the magazine. However, there is usually a chart providing the size conversion for different scales. Just as you would use these blueprints with wood or styrene you can also use them with paper that's been printed with an appropriate pattern such as wood, brick or metal. You can also create the model from wood and then mount appropriately printed paper on top.

You can cut from scratch or use a couple of different strategy to turn the blueprint into an actual scale size pattern. The "old school" way to increase a magazine blueprint to actual scale is to use the enlarge feature on a photocopier. A "modern day" alternative is to scan the blueprint using an all-in-one printer or take a picture of the blueprint using a digital camera or smartphone. You can then use one of several image editing programs to scale the blueprint to actual scale.

The advantage of digitally enlarging the blueprint is that you'll tend to get a better resolution on the final blueprint. It's also generally easier to split the model onto more than one piece of paper if necessary. It also gives you the opportunity to make modifications before printing out the blueprint. You can even turn the enlarged blueprint into a paper model kit by feeding printed paper into your printer and printing the blueprint on top of it. And, since you're working with paper rather than wood or plastic you can just re-print the model and start over if you get off track.

Real Life Photos

Photos of actual structures and landscapes is another inexpensive way to get started with building paper models. Most of today's smartphones have a high enough resolution camera to provide quality printed photos. The biggest challenge with real life photos is getting the scale correct. You'll most likely need to use an image editing program to resize the photo. Most of these programs have a ruler function that allows you to see the printed size as you work. You can either work in the inches to feet conversion for your scale or measure the actual size of an existing plastic building as a baseline.

The other major challenge is getting the photo level. A small slant becomes a big challenge once you begin to work with the photo in the editing software. Small slants can be corrected by rotating the image or using the perspective adjustment tool but too much modification will cause the image to pixelate at a certain point.

You'll usually want to take the photo at a distance to lessen the amount you'll need to scale the photo down. The exception to this would be specific details such as signs, trim etc. You may want to take to sets of shots: a full shot overall building and then separate close-ups of the detail elements. It's best to err on the side of taking too many photos rather than too few.

While working in the image editing software you may also want to crop or erase the unwanted elements or surrounding objects in the photo. This will save you some work when cutting the model out once it's printed.

Scenery Sheets

Scenery Sheets (www.scenerysheets.com) is designed to be a system for paper-based modeling. The system includes over two hundred different landscaping and structure elements such as grasses, waters, rocks, stones, roads, bricks, metals, etc. Each is professionally printed on an 80 lb. or 110 lb. cover stock paper, 8.5"x11" or 13"x19". Our standard 80 lb. sheets are approximately the thickness of the cover of this book. Each sheet features photo-realistic images with highlights and shadows to create the illusion of depth.

Each sheet is bled to the edge to eliminate the need to trim the pages and allow sheets to be placed end to end and top to bottom without seams. This allows modelers to combine multiple sheets to create walls, structures and landscapes of any size. The system includes both single sheets and full building and background kits. Kits feature the same patterns available in single sheets so modelers can combine elements from kits and single sheets to create truly custom structures and scenes.

They work for just about any sized project from a simple grass base or roadway to a large retaining wall or three-dimensional building. For added strength or depth they can be mounted to foam board, chipboard or wood.

To assist with structure building, there are also Scenery Sheets that contain architectural elements such as doors, windows, columns, etc.

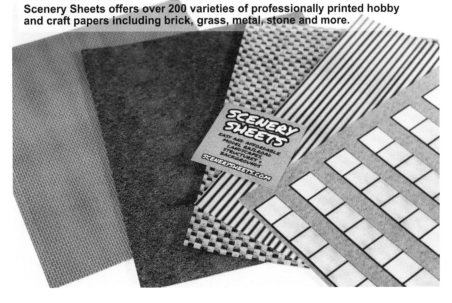

Scenery Sheets offers over 200 varieties of professionally printed hobby and craft papers including brick, grass, metal, stone and more.

Modelers can also purchase full kits to create stores, industrial buildings and more. All kits are based on existing sheets such as brick or stucco patterns. This makes it easy to customize building kits using additional sheets.

I created the few Scenery Sheet designs after experimenting with some of my wife's scrapbooking paper. I had used some brick sheets to create a retaining wall. Although it didn't look too bad, the issue with scrapbook paper is that it's generally not close to scale and the patterns didn't line up end to end so you could see the seams. Also, most scrapbook papers are printed on thin weight paper.

I started working on designs for brick sheets that were true to scale and did not show a seam when placed next to each other or overlapped. When it came time to print I decided early on that the product had to be professionally printed rather than just selling digital downloads that could be printed on an ink jet. Not only would professional printing increase the quality, it would allow me to print the sheet full to the edge.

Once I was satisfied with the brick I went to other materials including stone, rock, grass, water, metal and roads. Later when I started creating backgrounds and full kits I was careful to work with existing base designs such as the brick and stone. This ensured that the backgrounds and kits could be easily customized with additional sheets.

2

Basic Construction

Paper

Bases

Adhesives

Techniques

Overview

Paper based models are built on three main components: the paper, the base and the adhesive. (You can simplify this even further by using the paper itself as the base.) Constructing a model involves three basic actions: cutting, folding and gluing. In this chapter, we'll take a closer look at each of these components and actions. We'll also go over some troubleshooting strategies.

Paper

At the risk of stating the obvious, all paper models start with some type of paper. In some cases, the paper is printed with a construction material such as brick, stone or metal. In others, it's printed with a pattern such as the front, side or rear of a building. You'll usually be cutting a shape or pattern from a standard letter (8.5"x11") sheet of paper.

The main consideration in paper modeling is the thickness and finish on the paper. Thicker papers are generally sturdier for models but can be more difficult to fold or contour. Thicker paper also absorbs more ink creating richer colors and details. It's best to experiment with a few different variations to determine which works best for your needs.

However, there are a few rules of thumb. Thinner papers (20 lb. to 60 lb.) are better for base scenery such as grass or mountains. Medium thickness paper (80 lb.) is good if mounting to a base such as foam board or chipboard. Heavy thickness paper (110 lb. and above) should be used when creating the structure solely from paper (without a base).

Paper thickness is measured in pounds. This measurement is based on the weight of 500 sheets of the paper in its uncut state. There are several types of paper, each of which comes in several weights:

- Bond – Most common type of paper used for most home and office printing.
- Book – As the name implies this is a thinner paper used in book printing.
- Bristol – Heavier grade paper with a smooth finish used for paperback book covers.
- Cover – Heavy stiff paper used for folders, cards and book covers.
- Index – Stiff and inexpensive paper used mainly for index cards.
- Offset – Large rolls of paper used on printing presses.
- Tag – Dense strong paper used in the retail trade for product tags.
- Text – Thin paper generally used for flyers and announcements.

Take the gloss off pre-printed papers such as Scenery Sheets by applying diluted white glue or a clear coat.

Bond and cover stock paper is the most accessible to the average user. (In some cases, "pound" is represented the symbol "#" when referring to paper.) Bond paper is available from 20 lb. to 60 lb. Cover stock is available from 50 lb. to 130 lb. stock. Most photo papers fall somewhere the middle – around 50 to 60 lb. weight.

Most papers are available in a matt or gloss finish.

Matt finishes are less shiny but also less durable and may have dulled color. Gloss finishes are stronger, feature richer color and are less likely to fade. However, they may have a slight shine in certain light. This shine can be removed by applying a clear coat or even a thin coating of diluted white glue. You can also use the weathering techniques discussed later in the book.

If you're self-printing, it's also important to check the specifications of your printer to determine compatible thickness and finishes. Some thicknesses and coatings may jam the printer or may not allow the ink to soak in as well.

Bases

If you're not using paper that's at least 110 lb. or heavier, it's best to mount the paper on some type of base to give it additional strength and rigidity. Typical bases in paper modeling include foam board, chipboard, wood, matt board and Styrofoam.

Foam board is the most accessible, available at most hobby stores and even large discount stores. It typically comes in larger pieces and is semi-rigid but bendable. The biggest drawback of foam board is that it's sometimes frays when cut and can be prone to creasing.

Chipboard is a cardboard product that's available at some craft stores and most online craft supply websites. It comes in several different sizes and is generally flexible and easy to work with on projects. However, it often warps when used with white glue solutions. It can be flattened when placed under a weight overnight.

Paper-based scenery like brick or metal sheets are usually mounted to a base such as foam board, insulation, Styrofoam or chipboard. This provides stability and structure for walls and buildings.

The most common craft woods available are balsa wood and bass wood. Either makes a good base for paper modeling. Balsa wood is available in several thicknesses at most craft and hobby stores, bass wood must generally be ordered online. Balsa wood has been the product of choice for many modelers. The largest drawback is that it can be relatively expensive, especially when used for larger projects.

Matt board is generally used for mounting photographs but also makes a good base for paper modeling. It's very stiff and comes in several sizes. Matt board is often sold under the brand name Gatorboard. Matt board is one of the best products to use as a base. It cuts easily but provides a very rigid frame. However, it is probably the most expensive of all the bases – even Balsa wood.

Another option is Styrofoam. Styrofoam comes in several different densities. Light densities are useful for adding depth in backgrounds. Heavier densities are useful for three dimensional structures. Solid Styrofoam blocks are one of the easiest and strongest bases to the work with in paper modeling. The main drawback to using Styrofoam is that it does not allow structures to be lit since it is solid in the middle.

Choose the right base for the right job. You're bound to have a favorite but there are places where one type works better than another. Sometimes Styrofoam and wood can be too stiff and sometimes chipboard is too flexible. You may also need to vary your construction strategy. For example, if using chipboard with larger structures you'll most likely need to add inner supports. (We'll review structure building techniques in the next chapter.)

Base	Description	Cost	Variations	Advantages	Disadvantages	Applications
No base	(Un-mounted paper)	$	Thickness of paper	• Inexpensive • Less time • Tighter corners and seams	• Less strength • Harder to set	Self-printed pattern-based buildings with tabs
Foam board	Lightweight material composed of a foam core with paper faces	$	Sizes, colors and thicknesses	• Inexpensive • Easy to find • Easy to cut	• Paper face is acidic • Easily dented and bent	Backgrounds and walls
Chipboard	Pressed wood chips into a non-corrugated cardboard	$	Sizes	• Inexpensive • Easy to cut • Score-able and foldable	• Thinner than other bases • Can warp or bend	Small to mid-sized structures
Wood	Lightweight wood with coarse open grain	$$	Sizes and thicknesses	• Extremely strong yet lightweight	• More expensive • Harder to cut	Backgrounds, wall and larger structures
Matt board	Lightweight rigid display board with polystyrene core	$$$	Sizes and thicknesses	• Extremely strong • Moisture resistant	• Difficult to cut • Expensive	Backgrounds, walls, bases and larger structures
Styrofoam (sheets)	Close cell, extruded polystyrene foam	$$	Sizes and thicknesses	• Relative inexpensive • Lightweight	• Difficult to cut clean • Cracks and chips easily	Backgrounds and small walls
Styrofoam (solids)	Close cell, extruded polystyrene foam	$$$	Sizes and shapes	• Generally easy to work with • Strong and sturdy	• Large sizes can be expensive • Solid shapes can't be lighted	Structures of any size

Adhesives

The next important component in paper based modeling is the adhesive. You'll probably be working with less harsh adhesives than you have with plastic models. With paper modeling, the adhesive is more holding agent than a bonding agent. Plastic adhesives work on a chemical level to fuse the two plastic surfaces together. These chemical adhesives literally dissolve paper.

Working with paper allows you to utilize a much wider range of adhesives offering a range of different properties. In some applications, you'll be using a very precise line of glue; in other applications, you'll be painting or soaking the paper. You'll be working with more craft-based glues rather than the model glues. Look for white glues and clear glues marked as "photo safe." In short, get ready to visit the scrapbooking or card-making section of the of the craft store. (This is a good opportunity to get used to this area of the store, we'll be returning here a few more times.)

Diluting White Glue

When working with white glue, it's best to dilute it with water to make it easier to spread evenly on the paper. Diluted white glue also provides a thinner, smoother bond between the paper and the base.

Everyone has their own personal preference for the ratio of water to glue but most ratios range from 1 part water to 1 part glue to 4 parts water to 1 part glue. In most cases the amount of water is equal to or greater than the amount of glue. A higher water content in the mix makes the mixture more even and forgiving, while more glue makes it stick quicker.

One trick is to add a drop of dish washing detergent to the mix. This generally promotes the dispersion of the glue and water to create a more consistent mix.

Make Your Own Glue

White glue is a simple adhesive that you can make at home. Here are two recipes:

1. Heat 2oz of 2% milk and 1 tablespoon of distilled vinegar. Once the mixture curdles, pour it through a coffee filter. The vinegar reacts with a chemical in the milk to create an adhesive. Use a bit of baking soda with the curds to create right consistency.
2. Combine 1/3 cup of white flour and 2 tablespoons of sugar. Stir over low heat while gradually adding 1 cup of water.

These pastes can be mixed with varying amounts of water to achieve the desired consistency.

Simple white craft glue works in most paper modeling situations. These glues are often referred to as "white glue," "craft glue" or "school glue." White craft glues are water-based with a poly vinyl acetate to provide the stickiness. You can dilute these products with additional water to control the level of stickiness and create a "paintable" adhesive.

The craft company PLAID offers ModPodge, one of the most useful adhesives for paper craft and paper modeling. The product is basically a diluted white glue that comes in several different varieties. The ratio of glue to water is designed for paper crafts and the mixture stays stable much longer than a homemade diluted glue. It's stronger than normal white glues and can also be used as a sealer and finish.

Glue sticks are another popular adhesive usually found in school project applications. Although not always as strong as liquid glues they are easy to use, non-toxic and do not contain solvents. They generally work well when gluing paper scenery to chipboard and Styrofoam bases.

Wood glue is very similar to white glue but generally contains stronger adhesive elements. It dries faster and holds strong. Some paper modelers use wood glue for extra strength, however it tends to work best when using the paper with a base. Wood glue is also the natural choice if you're are using wood as the base for your structure.

You can use a variety of adhesives with paper models including diluted white glue, glue stick and spray adhesive. White glue is generally the most versatile.

3M Scotch® brand also offers a line of clear glue products that are photo safe. These products were originally designed for scrapbooking and card-making so they are safe to use with paper. These products are available in a variety of applicators, including a unit that comes with both a pen tip and a sponge tip.

You can also use spray adhesives in certain paper modeling applications. Spray adhesives make it easy to apply glue to larger surfaces. However, they tend to be messy and allow for only one application. Unlike white glues and clear glues the paper cannot be moved once applied.

Adhesive	Description	Advantages	Disadvantages	Applications
White glue	Water mixed with poly vinyl acetate	• Versatile • Easy to use • Repositionable	• Light immediate hold • Not as strong overall	Gluing paper to bases, smaller structures, large surface areas
Glue Stick	Varies by brand	• Clean and easy to use • Repositionable	• Not as strong overall	Gluing paper to bases such as chipboard and Styrofoam
Wood glue	Water mixed with poly vinyl acetate	• Stronger, longer hold • Easy to use	• Less versatile • Cannot be diluted	Self-printed models with tabs, gluing paper to wood bases
Clear glue (photo-safe)	Varies by brand	• Wide variety of applicators • Repositionable	• Hard to cover larger surfaces • Cannot be diluted	Structures of all sizes
Spray Adhesive	Chemical-based (trade secret)	• Quickly covers large areas • Strong hold	• Harsh chemicals • Not versatile or repositionable	Landscaping bases, large surface areas

Techniques

One of the nice things about paper modeling is that it generally does not require a wide range of techniques, especially to create basic structures. However, it's important to master the core set of techniques and approach them with special care and attention to detail. Creating paper-based models involves three basic actions: cutting, folding and gluing.

Cutting

To produce good paper model structures, you need to make neat, precise cuts along the pattern or shape. Any jagged edges, rips or miss-cuts will make the model look sloppy and create edges that are difficult to glue together. The best tool for cutting straight edges are slide and rotary style paper trimmers. (Guillotine style cutters don't work well because they're designed to cut several sheets at once.)

> **Paper Crafts**
>
> Paper modeling represents a relatively small percentage of the hobby industry. However, paper crafts such as scrapbooking and card making is an extremely popular hobby in American. That means that companies are constantly coming with new products and tools for these hobbyists. Almost anything developed for paper crafts is applicable to paper modeling. It's worth paying an occasional visit to these sections of your local craft store.

Curves must be cut with a blade-based hobby knife such as an X-ACTO knife. You can cut the straight edges with this type of knife as well but the paper trimmer saves some time, especially for larger models. Another option are the small scissors designed for papercraft, such as Cutter Bee precision scissors by EK Success. These scissors have a sharper, more fine edge then most scissors. They also have enhanced rubber grips.

There are a number things you should have in your toolbox for paper modeling including a paper trimmer, paint sponges bone knife, craft scissors, craft knife and more.

Whichever cutting tool you choose, it must be extremely sharp with a fine edge. You may also find yourself replacing blades more often than you did when cutting plastic. Although paper is thinner, it is much less tolerant of a dull or less fine edge. Replace or re-sharpen the blade as soon as you start to see any jagged edges or rips.

To cut bases you'll need a variety of tools based on the base. One of the advantages of chipboard is that you can cut it with the same tools you use for the paper. Straight edge modeling knives work best for foam board and wood. For matt board such as Gatorboard you'll want to invest in a matt cutter or Dremel tool to get a good clean edge. If you're cutting Styrofoam it's best to use cutting tools designed for that medium.

Often after cutting the paper you'll find some fraying or rough edges – these imperfections are usually very small but can still affect the look of the finished model. You can correct rough edges by running a precise cut craft scissor blade along the edge to remove the frayed paper and smooth the edge. Keep a light touch and angle the scissor blade towards the unprinted side of the paper. Rough edges on either the paper or a base can indicate your cutting blade is no longer sharp.

Folding

The art of the fold is one of the most overlooked but most important features in paper modeling. The quality of the fold affects the entire quality of the model. This is true for both gluing tabs and folds along a patterned sheet. All of your folds must be straight, crisp and firm. Follow these steps to achieve a good fold:

1. If a fold line does not already exist, *use a ruler or straight edge and a pencil to lightly mark the fold*. Do not try to fold paper without a guide line or by just using hash marks at either end.
2. *Use a bone folder or dull knife to score the fold*. A bone folder is a small plastic tool that's designed to make folds. They are available at most craft stores. Make sure the edge of the fold matches the pencil mark or pre-printed fold mark. Once the paper is scored you can use an eraser to remove the pencil mark.
3. *Carefully fold the paper along the score of the f*old. Fold the paper all the way over and press the fold down firmly with either the side of the bone folder or your finger.

Good folds take practice so try out some of folds on scrap paper or basic models before taking on a more complicated project.

Good Folds are the Key to Good Models

Use a straight edge such as a ruler and/or a bone knife to fold paper.

Mark the fold line on the back of the paper.

Use the straight edge or ruler to guide the fold.

Fold the paper over the straight edge or ruler several times.

A bone knife is a folding tool that can help you clarify your crease.

Make sure your folds are crisp, clean and well defined.

Gluing

Proper gluing technique is just as important in paper modeling as it is in plastic models. Over gluing soaks the paper and produces sloppy models. Under gluing allows the edges to separate. It's also important to make sure tabs, edges and bases are smoothly attached without any bumps or ripples.

Here are some strategies for gluing paper:

Paper Facts
• The US uses about 69 million tons of paper each year. • Recycled paper accounts for just over 1/3 of all paper making materials. • Paper can generally be recycled five to seven times before the fibers become too short. (Source: EPA.gov)

- Always work on top of a craft matt or other surface that resists adhesives. It's almost inevitable that you'll get some glue on the edge of the paper. You don't want the model to stick to your work surface.
- Use the right type of applicator for the situation: pen tip applicators or thin brushes for tabs and lines, sponge applicators and wide brushes for larger surfaces. Keep a tool box of different size brushes handy.
- For larger surfaces, spray a thin coating of water onto the paper to moisten it. This makes it easier to spread the glue. Note: this technique only works for water based glues such as white glue and wood glue.
- To make the paper and glue more flexibility and repositionable, dilute the glue with water. This keeps the adhesive from drying to quickly and gives you some additional play when lining up tabs and edges.
- Try to use just the right amount of glue for any application – bumps and ripples are usually the result of over gluing. Start conservative and add more glue if necessary.
- Make sure you get even coverage on the adhering surfaces and pay special attention to edges.
- Use a bone knife or paper craft smoothing tool to press remove any bubbles and flatten to the paper down along the tab, edge or base. Start from the middle and push firmly to the outer edges.
- Brush white diluted white glue on very evenly with no puddles to avoid bubbles - especially on flat surfaces.
- You can saturate the paper to help it conform to specific shapes. You can saturate and then still thin out the excess on the surface.
- One of the biggest issues with paper - especially if using diluted white glue - is curling or warping. Continue flatten or roll the paper down flat and be prepared with weights or clamps to hold the paper in place while drying. Curled or warped paper can always be correct by applying weight or working the paper back the other way. Chipboard also tends to curl or warp in this way.
- Cut printed sheets into smaller pieces and glue onto the base in layers to create a raised effect. Wash the area in diluted white glue and add a few pieces in random places. Repeat this multiple times, overlapping the pieces until the entire area is filled. The more you

repeat the process, the more layered the surface will look. The smaller the pieces, the more fine the layering.

- Be careful of sticky fingers…they can tear the paper or pull off printed graphics.
- When mounting on a base, mount prior to use in construction or on the layout. Use a flat surface where you can turn the base upside down and apply pressure to make sure the paper adheres flat to the base with no ripples. This is the most effective way to prevent ripples, even better than using the roller.

If you're working with a white glue, one of the other techniques you can use is sealing and finishing. Most white glues, properly diluted can spread on top of the paper to seal and finish the edges. This is most useful for landscaping, wall and extremely large structures such as multi-story buildings.

Use a brush to apply a thin layer of glue around the edges of the paper to smooth and weigh down any loose edges. The combination of the adhesive and coating makes the edges of the paper more difficult to spot. A coating of white glue can also take the shine off the paper coating for a duller or weathered appearance.

Essential Tools

Here's a list of tools no paper model builder should be without:

- ☐ Cutting matt
- ☐ Craft knife
- ☐ Precision scissors
- ☐ Paper trimmer
- ☐ Bone knife
- ☐ Glue brush applicator
- ☐ Thin paint brushes

3 Creating Structures

Background Structures

Free Standing Structures

Pre-created Models

Scratch Building

Overview

Once you've assembled all the right tools and gathered all the materials you're ready to get started. Regardless of the type of paper model, you'll want to find a nice flat workspace that's at least six to eight inches wider than the longest side of your model. You'll also need plenty of light and may even want to consider lighting designed for paper crafts.

Whether you're creating a flat front or three-dimensional model, it's best to cut everything out first – including the paper and base material – before starting to create the model. This allows you to review any directions and visual the pieces before construction. You may even want to take this opportunity to temporarily hold or place the pieces on your train layout.

Take this opportunity to determine if you need to make any modifications before starting the model. It's generally easier perform any trimming or extensions on the individual pieces before they're put together. If you trim equal amounts from opposite sides, even a pre-printed model can be modified. If you're working with a base, you can also extend models by adding additional sheets. We'll talk more about these operations later in this chapter.

Background Structures

If you're new to building paper models, background structures and flat fronts are a great way to get started. These types of structures can add a lot to a model railroad and are much less complex to build than free standing structures. (We'll also cover ¼, ½ and ¾ structures in this section.)

Flat backgrounds are on of the common uses of paper models. In this case the models are placed at slightly different distances from the wall to create more depth.

Background structures are one dimensional store fronts or other buildings that are mounted to a base and placed behind other structures on the layout. They are often mounted directly on the wall and produce the best effects when placed behind other three dimensional structures.

Creating a background model is straightforward, simply cut out the model and mount it to the base. There are two approaches to cutting the base: 1. Precut the base using the model as a guide. 2. Mount the model to the base and then trim to base to fit underneath it. The former is best for thicker bases such as foam board or wood. The latter works well with thinner bases such as chipboard.

The main consideration with background structures is the actual depth you want the building to stick out. It's best to have some type of gap between the flat front structure and the wall or rear of the layout. This helps to provide the illusion that's it a three-dimensional structure and that the layout continues. In the case of a flat structure the depth is determined mainly by the choice of base. You can increase the depth by creating multi-layer bases using several trimmed pieces of foam board, wood, etc.

Another option is to create ¼, ½ or ¾ depth buildings. This is a technique that plastic model builders have used for years. The idea is to create the front of the building and part of the side and roof but leave off the back of the building. The unfinished rear side goes right up against the wall or rear of the layout.

You can create a partial building from either a kit or scratch built building. To create one, simply cut the sides or pre-printed sheets to the desired depth, mount them on the base and attach the sides to the front. Attaching partial sides is generally easier than attaching full sides so this is another great way for the beginner to practice building.

When determining the right depth for background buildings, the best tool is line of sight. Simply put, line of sight refers to "who can see what objects and from what angle." In other words, if you're standing at a certain point what can you see and what can't you see on the layout. You theoretically only need to create what a visitor to your layout can see from various viewpoints.

You don't need to cover every possible viewpoint, just the viewpoints that your visitors are most likely to see. The best way to determine this is to view your layout from different sides and angles to determine the line of sight. You can use a long, thin and round piece of balsa wood to measure the line of sight.

> **Using Mirrors**
>
> One of the newer trends in model railroading is the use of mirrors to enhance backgrounds. In the past modelers have placed large mirrors across the entire layout to create the illusion of depth. However, today's model railroaders are bringing sophisticated refinements to this strategy by placing small mirrors in select areas to enhance specific scenes on their layout. For example, a mirror can be placed at the end of a street with the edges flanked on either side by false fronts. The mirror makes the street appear to go on indefinitely. Modelers are also using mirrors to extend track sidings and buildings. Just Google model railroad mirrors to see the latest examples.

Color one tip of the balsa wood with chalk. Start with the un-chalked side at the edge of your nose. Use the chalked tip to mark the point at the layout where your line of sight ends. Repeat this from several angles and use the chalk marks to determine how deep the false front buildings should come out from the wall or edge.

Free Standing Structures

As you might imagine, working with free standing paper model structures gets more complicated. Three dimensional structures built from paper present several challenges: getting the sides to stay up, tabs that won't quite stay together, sides that don't quite match up, paper sticking to your fingers, etc. It presents challenges that you might not necessarily face when working with plastic.

The best advice is patience and perseverance. It's best to take paper models one step at a time, taking a break or waiting for things to dry when necessary. It's also important to acknowledge and understand that your first couple of models probably won't turn out all that well. (Or at least you'll be less impressed with your first structure after you've completed a few others.)

General Tips

One of the biggest challenges when working with paper is holding the model together while you assemble the sides. The finished model collectively draws its strength for all four sides and the roof. Here are a few strategies you can use to hold things together when you've only completed a couple of sides:

- Use small, light modeling clamps and temporarily clamp the paper to wood
- Attach each side of the structure to the base before combining the sides
- Work with a solid base such as a Styrofoam or wood block
- Assemble the model on a floor or support base
- Assemble the model around some type of solid base during construction

When working with paper without a base material or a thin base material such as chipboard, you'll quickly notice the sides tend to bow in to the center of the model. The longer the sides, the more likely they are to bow. In this case, you'll need to provide some type of support for the model.

There are basically two options for support: build the model on some type of flooring or install cross beams through the center of the model. For the flooring, you can choose any of the base types discussed in the second chapter, although thicker bases provide more support and room for adhesive. If working with a floor, start by assembling the sides and then attach the sides to the floor.

You can use crossbeams to provide additional support for walls and structures. Crossbeams are usually necessary when using chipboard as a base but can also help with larger foam board.

For crossbeams, you can simply use the same base type as the rest of the model. Crossbeams should be attached approximately every four inches and are most effective when they run the entire height of the sides. A benefit to using crossbeams is that also provide support for the roof structure. For pitched roofs, make the crossbeams higher than the sides and match the cut angle to the pitch of the roof.

The roof itself is typically the most difficult aspect of any free-standing structure. The only exception are flat roofs which are relatively easy to install, especially if you're using crossbeams or a solid base. Pitched roofs are easier if you size the crossbeams to support them, or use tabs to attach them to the inside of the front and back of the model.

The most challenging roofs are multi-pitch roofs and roofs with gables or other architectural bump outs. An example of a multi-pitch roof would be a railroad station with both a front and back pitch and a pitch at the sides. This type of roof would require eight folds, each of which most hold together precisely for the roof to sit properly on top of the sides.

The best strategy for this type of roof is start with the main fold along the center, then work symmetrically on the other folds. If your second fold is the upper right, the third fold should be the lower left. This strategy keeps the roof balanced and reduces the strain from the completed sides.

The other nuance of multi-pitch roofs is that the tabs should not be folded at ninety degree angles like the sides. Instead, fold the tabs to the same angle as the pitch of the roof. If the roof section has a sixty-degree pitch, fold the tab sixty degrees in the other direction. This will allow the fold to line up with the pitch of the adjoining roof section.

With free standing structures, it's especially important to follow the strategies and utilize the tools presented in the second chapter. Take time to get all the folds right and err on the side of too little adhesive rather than too much. You can always add more adhesive; you can't easily take adhesive away.

Start with smaller structures with a basic shape such as a square or rectangle. Avoid models with complex shapes and bump outs until you've mastered the basics. One of the advantages of working with paper is that it's less expensive and more forgiving than plastic. If things get too far out of hand, you can always just start over.

Working with Pre-Created Models

Pre-created models such as those available for download on the Internet take much of the guess work out of free standing structures. They offer models that have already been measured out and tested. They also usually include pictures of the finished product. Most also include tabs, a luxury you won't have with scratch built models unless you build them into your design.

Always read all the instructions before starting a pre-created model. It's an obvious statement but well worth repeating here. Looking ahead in the instructions allows to anticipate upcoming steps that may rely on doing earlier steps a certain way. It also allows you to plan ahead for natural

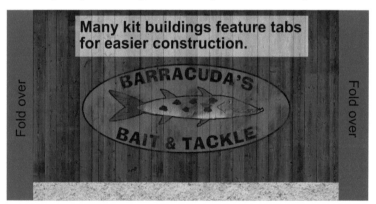

stopping points. Unlike a plastic model which will generally stand up under its own power relatively early in the build, it may be several steps before a paper model is at a point where you can safely stop work.

As mentioned above, one of the greatest advantages of pre-created models is that they generally include tabs for attaching the sides. However, used incorrectly tabs can be more of a hindrance. To work properly, tabs must be folded extremely precise and clean. Any deviation from the fold line between the side and the tab will result in a crooked model. Also, once a tab is folded incorrectly it's very difficult to correct it. The original seam will remain and weaken the corrected fold.

Consider using a folding tool such as a bone knife to fold the tabs on your model. An alternative is to press a straight edge such as a ruler down on the fold line between the tab and the side. Use the bone knife or straight edge to apply just enough pressure to make an indentation along the fold line. Be careful not to exert too much pressure or you'll rip or weaken the paper.

Once you've created the indentation, the paper should naturally fold along this line. For larger tabs, fold around the bone knife or straight edge. Regardless of the size of the tab, it's best to fold the entire tab over at once rather than a section at a time. This will create one solid fold that's consistent along the entire line. If you do end up with a messy, crooked or inconsistent fold it's easier to just re-print that side of the model rather to try and correct the fold.

Although the idea behind a pre-created model is to build that exact model, it is possible to customize these types of structures. In most cases, pre-created models are sold as digital downloads. This allows you to print the pieces of the model as many times as necessary. That makes it easy to extend the model if you need to fill a larger footprint than the original model.

Model kits from Scenery Sheets are designed to be customized along at least one or more dimensions. You can trim the sides to fit your exact specifications and in some cases the front and backs of kits are also modifiable. If you plan to trim a model down to a smaller size, always plan your modifications ahead of time and make your cuts before mounting the paper to a base.

When extended the model by printing additional pages, cut the extension with an additional twenty percent on each. This essentially creates a tab on each side that you can use to overlap the original side or piece. Also, it's better to extend the model in the middle rather than at the edge since an extension at the edge – particularly a smaller one – will weaken the connection between the two sides. You can also strengthen the extension by applying a base.

Just as you can extend the model by printing extra pages, you can also trim the model down by cutting the sides or pieces and then reattaching them. Make the cut at the end of the side. Just remember to leave about twenty percent more than you need to provide a tab to attach the sides.

One way to hide seams, especially on corners is to fold and place a trim piece along the seam.

Scratch Building

Pre-created models are a great way to get started with paper modeling. However, scratch building allows you to take full advantage of the customizable nature of working with paper. Just as with plastic, you can design a specialized structure to fit the exact dimensions you need on the layout. You can also re-create any type of industry or theme. Unlike plastic, paper is more affordable and more forgiving.

Like any other type of model, you'll want to do some degree of planning before you start building. However, the nature of paper does allow for more improvising than plastic structures. If you don't like something, you can always just rebuild it again. One strategy is experiment with partial builds – two or three sides attached together or just a flat front structure.

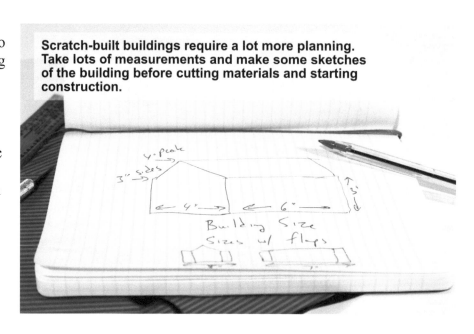

Scratch-built buildings require a lot more planning. Take lots of measurements and make some sketches of the building before cutting materials and starting construction.

In most cases, you'll at least want to measure the footprint of the building. You can always play around with height, color, texture, etc. but the area of the structure is probably set based on the surrounding elements on the layout. Determine the length and width, as well as any special shaping or "bump-outs."

Will the building a be simple rectangle or a more complex shape such as a "T" or cross? Will the sides be flat or have vestibules or overhangs? These items should really be worked out before you start building because you'll want to plan supports and tabs for attaching these areas. You also need to make sure the area on the layout can accommodate these features and that they'll look right in that placement.

One of the best ways to plan a design while still maintain some room for improvisation is to create a mock-up. This strategy is already practiced by some plastic scratch builders. The idea is to create the basic shape of the model using plain copy paper. Follow on the same cutting and gluing strategies covered earlier in the book – just keep in mind you don't need to be exact.

The idea of a mock up is to get an idea of how the structure will look in the over scene, not necessarily create every detail of the building. One option is to create a mockup of just the floor of the building. This is a quick and easy way to see how well the footprint of the building fits in the area. Another option is to use a base material to create the footprint of the building, then use this piece as the floor of the building.

If you plan to work with a base, you can even create the entire shape of the building first, then cover it with the printed paper. One advantage to this strategy is that you can perfect the shape of the structure without worrying about stressing or tearing the paper. It's also easier to correct mistakes or change the design as you go since you don't have to realign the pattern on the paper.

One of the biggest challenges is scratch building is the lack of tabs that usually come with most pre-created models. The biggest remedy is to create your own tabs by allowing about twenty-percent extra space on each piece of paper. You can then fold this extra space over using the folding techniques reviewed earlier in this book. This strategy also ensures that your model will not have seams where the sides come together.

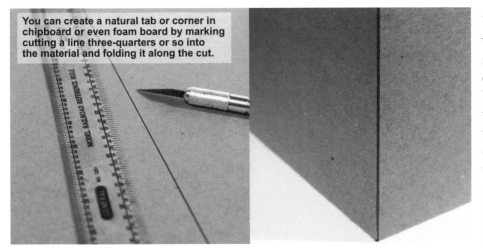

You can create a natural tab or corner in chipboard or even foam board by marking cutting a line three-quarters or so into the material and folding it along the cut.

You can also create tabs in thinner bases such as chipboard. To create a tab, score the base by making a three-quarter cut into the material using a craft knife or paper trimmer. Use a straight edge to create a cut line first, then cut closely along the line. As with the paper itself, leave about twenty percent of the material as the tab. Once you score the material, you should be able to fold it over.

Scoring bases such as chipboard is an effective way to create partial models that stand on their own. However, the drawback is that a folded base creates a larger seam or gap where the two sides come together. The existence of seams or gaps along the sides is a general problem with most scratch built models. Getting the paper to come together at the seams is one of the largest challenges you'll face when building these structures.

Luckily there is a relatively simple fix. Instead of trying to get two pieces of paper to come together perfectly where the two sides come together, simply fold the paper over the seam. When cutting the paper, leave about ten to twenty percent extra for the fold over the scene. Use the same folding tools and techniques to get a quality fold over the joining of the two sides.

Once the first piece of paper is folded and adhered over the seam, overlap another piece of paper to cover the rest of the side. Seams are generally less visible when not placed at the corner. Also, it's generally easier to line up sheets on a side rather than at a corner. You can even seal the seam with a coating of diluted white glue to further camouflage it.

This strategy works best if you fold the paper over the front and back of the building and leave the seams on the sides. (In most cases the sides of your building will be less visible on the layout since they're likely to be facing or up against another building.)

You can give edges and corners a cleaner look by measuring the paper so its long enough to fold over.

4

Creating
Scenery

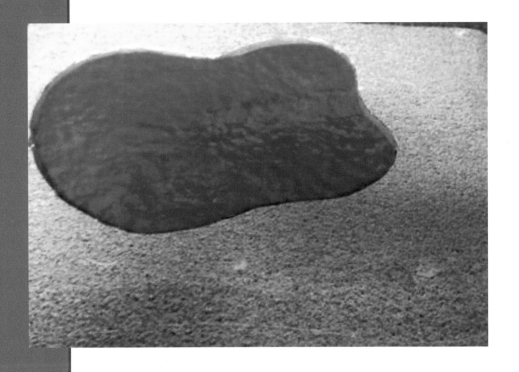

Paper as a Starting Point

Landscaping Strategies

Forests and Hills

Grade crossings and Portals

Overview

When it comes to paper modeling, most people think of structures and objects. However, paper is also a great resource in landscaping your model railroad layout. Landscaping includes grass, asphalt, water, rocks, mountains and just about anything else that sits under or over your track and structures.

Like the flat front models discussed earlier in this book, landscaping applications are an easy way to get started with paper in model railroading. I first discovered the paper modeling products while accompanying my wife on frequent trips to the craft store to purchase scrapbooking supplies. Scrapbook paper comes in hundreds of patterns including brick, metal, grass and more.

It wasn't long before I tried using a few sheets of brick paper to create a retaining wall on our store display layout. I mounted the brick sheets to a strip of foam board and then mounted that strip of foam board to the wood frame of the upper deck of the layout. The results were okay, but the real pay-off was discovered the potential of using paper to landscape a train layout.

Craft Store Items

These are some items that you should regular browse for in craft or scrapbooking stores:

- ☐ Textured papers
- ☐ Embellishments
- ☐ Vintage ads and signs
- ☐ Die-cut items such as trims and other details
- ☐ Stickers and vinyl shapes
- ☐ Tools such as cutters, bone knifes, etc.
- ☐ Specialized adhesives with textures and other effects
- ☐ Markers and pens for weathering

Once you start working with retaining walls, it's a pretty short leap to flat front buildings and then an even shorter jump to three dimensional structures. However, you'll quickly discover three major drawbacks with paper designed for scrapbooking: it's very difficult to find anything to scale, it's generally relatively thin and it's not designed to "tile." In other words, you can't line up multiple sheets without creating a seam in the image.

Many of the key advantages of the Scenery Sheets line grew out of a need to correct these flaws. The sheets are designed to scale, printed on thicker paper and can be placed end to end and top to bottom without creating a seam. That said, I still browse the scrapbooking area of the craft store from time to time for inspiration.

For example, there's a scrapbook paper made of cork that can be used to simulate several types of landscaping such as a dried-up river bed or dry field. You can also find papers that look like metal, some even with the ripples that you'd find on a corrugated roof. Water is another substance that's easy to simulate with the right paper – just look for something with the right color and a bit of a swirl or sheen to it.

Paper as a Starting Point

When it comes to landscaping on your model railroad, the most useful application for paper is as a starting point. Even a small layout generally requires a fair amount of landscaping. A 4x6 train layout requires a total of 24 square feet of landscaping and that's without considering mountains or other three dimensional formations. That's a lot of grass and/or asphalt to put down. The traditional way to address this requirement is paint or rolled grass paper.

Paper provides an alternative with a lot more options and flexibility. You can find paper products that simulate grass, water, sand, roads and just about anything else you can imagine on your layout. It's also cheaper, easier and less messy to work with than most paints and rolled grass mats. Just like paint or grass mats you can apply other scenery products on top of it.

This also allows you to save money on foams and lichens. A layer of paper provides a baseline of color and texture that does not require nearly as much foam or lichen to create the same effect. Paint provides a layer of color but it does not typically include any texture. You can apply foam and lichen to paper by giving the paper a "white-wash" with diluted white glue.

A notable exception to this are the textured spray paints produced by some manufactures. The darker blacks and grays work well on bridges to simulate metal…you can also use the textured reds and oranges to add rust. The greens and tans can be used for grass and sand

Trees and Bushes
All this talk of using paper in model railroad landscaping begs the question: Can you create trees and bushes from paper? The short answer is "no" - at least not in terms of anything that has a level of realism. That said, if your layout has a more tinplate or "Plasticville" style look there are two methods for creating "stylistic" trees.

1. Glue two pieces of grass paper back to back and the then cut two equal sized triangles out of the resulting double-sided piece. Cut a slit in the top center of each triangle and then slide one triangle perpendicular into the other.
2. Glue two pieces of grass paper back to back and then cut into smaller squares. Paint the resulting double sided squares with diluted white glue until saturated. Crumple and form the squares into a ball to create the shape of the tree.

Use a round piece of balsa wood or actual small stick to create the trunk of the tree or bush. |

respectively but tend to have a look more suited to traditional snap together houses rather than high-rail or realistic scenes.

You can soak paper scenery in diluted white glue and then mold it to foam board, crumpled newspaper, etc. to create hills and mountains.

Another use for paper is as temporary landscaping to provide a semi-finished look to the layout while more in-depth scenery is applied. Your layout will have a more polished look and you'll be able to visualize the way certain colors and textures will look with the surrounding scenery.

Another way paper demonstrates its flexibility in railroad scenery is the ability to turn almost any page into papier-mâché. Traditional papier-mâché soaks plain white or tan strips of paper in a glue solution to create a thin plaster. You can substitute printed paper for the plain white paper to produce a plaster that already has a base of color and texture.

If you're working with a paper that's 80 lb. weight or less, you can heavily paint or soak the paper with a diluted white glue or Modge Podge to create a pliable product that can be laid directly on top of wire or cardboard supports. Once the paper becomes soaked with the glue it can easily be contoured to any shape. Again, this is an effective way to create a base of color and texture. Foam and lichen products can then be added to create an even more realistic look.

Landscaping Strategies

Applying adhesive

The second chapter of this book presented a wide range of adhesives. When working with paper in landscaping applications such as grass or pavement diluted white glue is almost always the best choice. It provides the most flexibility and allows for adjustment before the paper completely sets up. White glue can be mixed with water to create varying levels of "tackiness." It can also be applied in different amounts to increase or decrease the pliability of the paper.

It's best to experiment with different ratios of glue to water and more or less glue on a small area to get the right mix. The right mix will change from scene to scene based on the contour. Apply the glue with a soft-bristled paint brush – you may even want to invest in artist brushes rather than standard home improvement brushes. Smooth the paper down as you go with a bone knife, straight edge or similar tool.

Minimizing seams

One of the biggest issues when working with paper scenery are the inevitable seams that will occur where individual sheets or pages meet or overlap. Even if the paper is designed to create a seamless texture or pattern, you'll still be able to see where some of the individual sheets come together. The main factor with seams is the strength and angle of the lighting on the train layout.

Reduce or hide seams by white-washing them with a coat of diluted glue. This also prevents the edges from peeling.

Luckily, you can minimize almost any seam by applying a wash of diluted white glue over top of the area or even across the entire area. (If you plan to add foam or lichen you'll be applying a wash over the paper anyway.) This application of white glue seals the seam and takes the shine off the paper to prevent the lighting from calling attention to the seam.

Dealing with edges

Another issue you'll come across is dealing with an area where two types of landscaping come together. An example of this would be an area of grass meeting an area of dirt or sand. You can always cut the edge of the paper but in general it can be difficult to create a truly natural looking seam. There are three strategies for dealing with edges:

- Hide the edges – Design your layout with the edges of scenes in mind and use track, walls and structures to hide the point where one type of scenery ends and another begins. Example: use grass paper on one side of the track and dirt paper on the other side of the track.

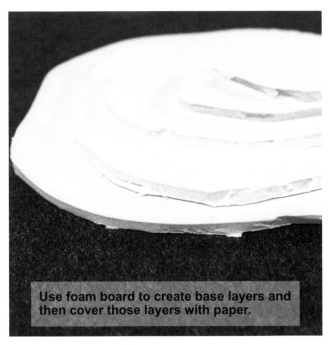

In this case the track is used as a natural delineator and cover the seam between the grass and asphalt.

- Cover the edges – Apply complimentary colored foam or lichen products along the edge to ease the transition between the two scenes and create some "bleed" between the two scenes. Example: apply small green foam pieces on top of the grass paper and on some of the dirt paper.
- Cut the edges – Cut a jagged or even edge along one of the paper edges to create a more natural transition using a craft knife or one or more specialized scrapbooking edge scissors available in craft stores. Example: cut the edge of the grass scene with patterned edge scissors several times at different angles.

Use foam board to create base layers and then cover those layers with paper.

Creating contours and levels

The most obvious drawback to paper is that it's generally flat. It is possible to buy printed papers that have some texture or print downloaded designs on textured paper. However, these tend to be more expensive options and the texture tends to be generic. In other words, the individual elements of the print such as bricks aren't raised; the paper simply contains a cross-weave or similar texture.

Well-designed scenery paper designs create the illusion of depth using subtle details and shadows in the print. You can take this another step further on the layout by creating contours and levels whenever possible. You'll want to establish pitches and inclines with cardboard frames or foam before laying down the paper. Plan on some creating some rolling hills or contours in different areas. Even simply raising one whole area up can make a huge impact.

For example, if you have a grass area next to a dirt area or water area, make the grass area a fraction of an inch higher. You can also use a bit of foam or lichen to smooth over the edge of the raised area. Town and city scenes lend themselves especially well to this strategy. Use a piece of foam board or wood to raise the town or city blocks higher than the roads. Chapter six of this book focuses on these types of strategies more deeply.

Specific Scenes

Flatlands and Hills

The flatter areas of your layout are a good place to start experimenting with paper in landscaping. It's relatively easy to apply paper sheets to these areas and you can cover up mistakes with additional paper. Paper is an effective way to lay down basic ground cover such as grass, sand or pavement. It's an excellent way to visualize the various scenery areas of your layout.

As mentioned in the previous section, consider building up or lowering areas of the layout using other materials or cutting away some of your underlayment (such as Styrofoam or creosote). If you're using bench work construction on your layout, you would need to build up the gaps between the track anyway. Paper works well as a covering for all the traditional ways of creating contours on a model train layout:

- Cardboard and newspaper
- Wire screening
- Sculpted foam

The only difference when working with paper is that you'll want to make the contours as smooth as possible so the paper lays on top easier. Paper will generally be less tolerant if you have small bumps or ridges. However, you can remedy this to a certain extent by soaking the paper with more glue and using more water in the glue/water mix. That will make it easier to form fit the paper to the exact contour.

One of the advantages of paper is that you can add it before or after laying your track since it's easy to cut and shape. You can even slip the paper underneath it if you're using track with integrated roadbed such as Lionel Fastrack or Bachmann EZTrack. There is no necessarily right or wrong way to work with paper, just different effects.

When working with flatlands and hills you'll almost certainly want to use a diluted white glue solution to smooth and seal the edges – or even the whole page. However, different ratios of water to glue produces different effects. Using a high ratio of water to glue will result in a completely smooth effect on the paper. Using a higher ratio of glue produces a rough or grainy feel to the paper.

You may also choose to leave the paper on its own or enhance it with foam or lichen scenery products. These products can be applied immediately after you paint the sealant coat of glue or you can always glue as you go later. If adding foam or lichen immediately you'll need to keep a higher ratio of glue to water to make sure the scenery material adheres properly.

One of the keys to making paper scenery look good is to vary the texture types throughout the layout. Designate some areas as grass, others as sand, water, pavement, etc. If possible, use different shades of grass, sand, etc. in different areas. As mentioned above, track can be a good way to hide the transitions between these different textures.

An effective strategy is to lay your track first and then designed on the textures for each area, making sure that most areas start and end under the track. Again, track with built in roadbed is ideal because it provides a wider surface area to conceal the seams where two texture types come together.

Another technique is to lay down a covering of the most dominant texture first. For example, if you think most of your ground coverage will be dirt or sand cover the entire base of the layout with that texture first. If your train layout is dominated by track with lots of yard space, industry sidings, reverse loops, etc. you may want to cover the entire base with pavement or concrete.

Because the paper provides a relatively thin base and is easy to glue you can simply layer the other scenery areas on top of the base. Follow the edging techniques discussed earlier in this chapter to minimize the transition between areas. Also, it's best to use a higher ratio of glue to water when adding a second layer. Two much water and you'll over soak the layers and causing bleeding of the colors.

Roads and Grade Crossings

Soak paper in diluted glue and then mold over track roadbed to easily create railroad crossings.

Roads and grade crossings are a natural fit for paper-based scenery because they are generally flatter and involve straight lines. Road and asphalt-based projects another great way to get started with paper-based modeling. Laying down roadway is often as simple as cutting it out and gluing it down. This is particularly true for city streets which tend to be straight and flat.

In a city or town scene, paved roads are typically the lowest point or may be raised slightly above the ground. For this reason, you can glue streets directly to the base of the layout or a grass or asphalt covering. Chipboard is a perfect base to raise the street slightly above the ground. If you're using foam or lichen to add texture to the ground, make sure you lay down the streets first to avoid bumps.

Rural streets tend to be bit rougher and uneven. You probably want to start with a surface that's slightly uneven or even a bit bumpy before laying down the paper. Again, use additional water and soak the paper more heavily with the glue/water solution. Do not use a stiff base like chipboard in this case.

Another strategy is to allow bumps, creases and ripples to occur when you lay down the paper roads or asphalt. Normally you would use a bone knife or other tool to smooth these issue down, but they can add character in certain situations. This is also true for ground cover such as grass or sand, although in these cases you'll probably want to enhance the bumps and ripples with foam or lichen.

Grade crossings are another great use for paper modeling and an excellent starter project. Paper allows you to make any section of track – straight or curved – into a grade crossing and you can vary the location and angle of the crossing. (Most pre-fabricated crossings are designed to sit in the center of the track piece and sit perpendicular to the track.)

If the track does not have a built-in roadbed, you'll want to mount the paper roadway to a base such as chipboard before installing it. If the track does have built in road bed – such as Lionel Fastrack or Bachmann EZTrack – you can mount the paper roadway directly to the roadbed surface. You'll need to cut the road surface into three or four segments according to the scale and type of track.

For two rail track you'll have a section leading up to the track, a section leading away from the track and a section in between the rails. For three rail track you'll have sections leading up to and away from the track as well as two equidistant sections on either side of the center rail. Measure the distance between the rails to determine the width of the small segments.

Glue down the roadway around the grade crossing first, allowing for some overlap between the pieces leading up to and away from the crossing. Next add the pieces on the outside of the rails. Use diluted white glue to seal the seams between the sections of roadway. The last step is to glue down the small sections between the rails.

Mountains and Valleys

As mentioned earlier in this book, you can use paper as a substitute in papier-mâché mixes to create larger hills and mountains on your model train layout. You can also simply soak the pages in diluted white glue and lay them down directly on your cardboard framework or wire mesh. When creating these types of formations, you may want to allow the paper to bump and ripple rather than smooth it flat. This provides additional character to the surface of the hill or mountain.

Unlike many paper scenery projects, mountains do require a bit more planning. It's difficult to improvise a mountain formation. You should draw out the footprint on the base of the layout and determine the heights at various points. The entire footprint and the overall shape must be fully reflected in the superstructure of the model. The paper will only provide a finished surface.

You won't be able to sculpt out contours and features as you can with foam or spackling. However, you can use the paper to provide a finished look or pre-colored base to foam or spackle.

Like roads, retaining walls are another natural fit for paper modeling. Creating a retaining wall is as simple as mounting the paper to the base and then mounting the base to the back wall or mountain side. If mounting the retaining wall to a mountain, be sure to plan the flat surface into the design of the mountain superstructure.

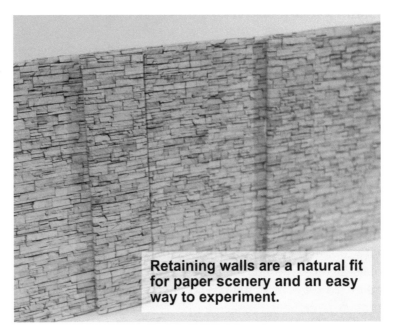

Retaining walls are a natural fit for paper scenery and an easy way to experiment.

For a straight retaining wall you can use almost any base from chipboard to foam to wood. For a curved retaining wall you should use a flexible base such as chipboard or simply print the pattern on thicker paper (110 lb. or greater). In most cases 80 lb. paper mounted on chipboard is the ideal solution.

The chipboard provides a degree of stability to the wall while still allowing it to bend. There are several ways to ensure a curved wall stands up:

- Mount it to the curved superstructure of a mountain
- Cut a slit in the Styrofoam or creosote base of the layout and glue the wall into it
- Attach chipboard or wood bases along the back of the wall
- Clamp the wall in a curved position and leave for several days

Tunnel portals are another natural fit for paper-based modeling. Like grade crossings, this is another area of modeling where you are fairly bound by available products on the market. Most portals and their openings are set sizes and designed to fit a straight piece of track. With plastic or foam product portals you're also limited to a narrow range of stone or notched concrete styles.

You can create paper-based tunnel portal out of just about any pattern available including stone, rock, brick, concrete, etc. You can also custom cut the shape, size and opening to accommodate the specific needs of your layout. Like any other paper model, portals can be mounted to any base. However, it's usually most effective to mount the portal to a thicker base such as Styrofoam or wood.

Follow these steps to create custom tunnel portals:

1. Measure the location of the portal and pre-cut the whole in the retaining wall or mountain side. Make sure the hole is large enough to accommodate the entire portal, not just the portal opening. It's also best to make it a tight fit.
2. Use the measurements from step one to cut the shape of the portal including the opening out of the base material. Test the base in the opening to make sure it's a good fit and make any necessary adjustments or recut the base.
3. Once you're sure about the shape of the base, cover the base in the paper. Keep in mind that you can use the pattern on the paper in a variety of ways to create different effects. For example, you can cut concrete printed paper into rectangles to create cement blocks.

The application of paper in model railroad scenery is only limited by imagination. One of the more "out of the box" strategies is to use paper and thicker bases such as wood or Styrofoam to create trestles. A lot of model railroaders already use cut wood pieces to create custom inclines and raised sections of track. These wood pieces can easily be covered with paper scenery products to create a finished look.

Use an adhesive appropriate for the base. For example, use wood glue when attaching the paper to wood blocks. In most cases, you'll also want to make sure that you smooth the paper down using a straight edge or other tool. Not only do ripples and bubbles look unrealistic in these situations, they'll increase the likelihood that the paper will eventually peel away from the base.

5 Creating Depth

Layering Opportunities

Details and Enhancements

Forced Perspective

Weathering

Overview

Because paper is essentially a flat medium, modeling with paper often involves creating the illusion of depth. In many cases this depth is built right into the image on the paper. Varying colors, lighting and shadows make a flat picture appear to have dimension. For example, paper imprinted with a brick pattern usually includes shadowing or darkening to make the bricks appear higher than the mortar.

The illusion is not that far-fetched when you consider that a scale brick would only be a very small fraction of an inch higher than the mortar anyway. If you examine a plastic brick panel or scale brick building, you'll find that the bricks are merely an imprint or stamp a couple of millimeters high. The case is the same for wood, stone and other textures. If you're working with paper printed with a photo-realistic image you need to get fairly close before you can notice the difference between it and a plastic or wood structure.

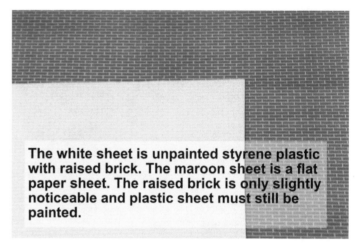

The white sheet is unpainted styrene plastic with raised brick. The maroon sheet is a flat paper sheet. The raised brick is only slightly noticeable and plastic sheet must still be painted.

Beyond the imprint on the paper, there are several additional techniques and strategies you can employ to increase the illusion of depth. In most cases the only limitations to these methods are your own imagination, patience and time. Like most other model railroading projects, you can continue to enhance over time. You'll often find inspiration striking long after you've completed a basic model. Because paper is relatively forgiving and flexible as a medium you can usually add to it easily.

Layering Opportunities

The most basic way to increase the overall depth is to increase the number of bases. Instead of working with one flat base beyond the entire paper model, use several layers of bases. For example, if you're building a road vary the number of chipboard pieces underneath different sections to raise and lower it. In many cases an opportunity for layers naturally presents itself.

Sidewalks offer a perfect opportunity to apply layering on your layout.

SEASONS' FLOWER SHOP

One of the best examples is town or city blocks. Sidewalks and building foundations are almost always raised slightly from street level. (Rural areas are an exception to the rule.) It's easy to make a city or town scene "pop" just by adding an extra layer of foam board or wood underneath the area with the sidewalks and buildings. This lowers the street level and simulates curbs. You'll want to wrap the sidewalk/building layer with a concrete or similar pattern to provide a color base. This ensures all the edges or curb areas are covered.

When planning or working with your layout, keep an eye out for other areas that naturally lend themselves to different levels. Water is another natural choice since most bodies of water sit lower than the surrounding land. Again, just adding a extra layer of foam board, Styrofoam or wood can make all the difference. Here are some other opportunities for layers:

- Gravel pits
- Maintenance areas
- Swimming pools
- Parking lots
- Sports fields
- Station areas
- Construction sites

Easily create a layered effect with stone by cutting the paper into small pieces and gluing them onto the base. White wash the surface with diluted white glue to seal it.

If you're building a rock retaining wall, deliberately vary the thickness of the wall or the overall shape. An even more advanced technique is to vary the thickness of the base under individual rows or sections. You can cut a piece of rock wall printed paper into several strips that correspond to the rows of rock. Mount these strips onto bases of varying thicknesses. One easy way to do this is to use chipboard and creating different thicknesses by using more than one layer of chipboard. After you've mounted all the individual strips, mount each strip onto a master base to hold the entire pattern.

You can use a similar strategy with roofing such as shingles or metal sheets. Instead of just mounting the whole page to the base, cut the page into strips along the shingles or metal strips.

The store front of this building has been bumped out and the windows inset to create more depth.

Start at the bottom of the roof and glue one strip at a time, positioning the next strip so that it slightly overlaps the previous strip. This creates an effect that looks like real shingle or roof panels. In this case, you do not even need to vary the thickness; the overlap itself is enough to create the affect.

Buildings and structures also lend themselves to layering in several ways. Interiors are the most obvious. The easiest way to assemble a building is to either use windows that are pre-printed on the design on simply glue windows on top of the paper sides. However, you can create a more layered affect by cutting out all the windows and using set back interiors. On the most basic level you can cut out the windows and glue them underneath the paper rather than on top of the paper.

Another alternative is to cut out all the glass areas from the windows and replace these areas with clear cellophane or a similar material. This strategy also allows you to add lighting to the building. (Note that this strategy will not work with a solid base such as a Styrofoam block.) You can also add blinds or curtains over all or parts of the windows. Depending on the building you will need to add some type of material or at least make sure the inside of the building is covered in a dark neutral color.

You can take things a step further using a detailed interior and placing that interior slightly set back inside the building. The amount the interior should be set back is relative the building's position on the layout. The closer to the edge, the further you need to set back the interior to create the right affect. Buildings in the rear of the layout need only a slight setback to create the layered affect. The best approach is to assemble the entire outside structure of the building and then test the visual effect of placing the interior at different positions within the building.

Building trim pieces also present opportunities for depth. If your building has columns, you can cut out the columns, mount them on a base material and then glue that base to the front or side of the building. You can also create a three-dimensional column by gluing four column sides together. Some manufacturers such as Scenery Sheets provide 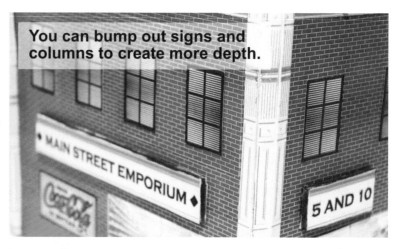 architectural detail sheets with elements like columns. If you're working with a downloadable model, print the model multiple times to get the additional columns.

You can do this with just about any piece of building trim including columns, railings, steps, brackets, etc. These strategies also work with vestibules and steps. Cut these elements out of the model and then mount them to their own bases before re-attaching them to the building front or side. An alternative to cutting the elements out is to use two or more copies of the model. Use the first model as template for arranging the elements in the correct places and the second model as a source for the trim pieces. In most cases you can purchase two copies of a paper building for less than the cost of one plastic model.

Details and Enhancements

Model railroaders have long used small detail parts to enhance plastic structures – both in scratch building and on built up models. Only a few high-priced kits offer a structure that contains a fully realized structure out of the box. Usually you need to purchase additional details such as chimneys, vents, downspouts, railings, etc. to achieve the best affect. These elements can have the same effect on a paper structure as well.

If you're working with photorealistic paper materials or paper model kits you can "plus" the model by adding paper or plastic details. These elements go a long way to making your structure look more realistic and add to the effect of making a flat structure look three dimensional. Many of the details can be constructed from paper to keep costs down. Here are some suggestions:

- *Signage* – Signs are one of the easiest ways to enhance using paper. Print out the sign and mount it to a base such as chipboard, foam board or wood. You can either mount the sign to the front of the building or attach it to a small diameter piece of balsa wood or plastic to create a sign that hangs perpendicular to the building.

Sometimes a simple awning is enough to add a bit of depth to a building.

- *House numbers* – House numbers are a simple detail that you can mount on a thin base and glue to the front of the house. In many cases, you can even use peel and stick letters if they are the correct scale.

- *Awnings* – It's relatively easy to fashion an awning from paper. Start with a strip of paper with some type of pattern (in many cases blinds or metal patterns can double as awnings) and cut 45 degree slits at each corner. Fold the ends over at the cut to create triangle forms on each end. Awnings don't necessarily need to be mounted to bases. Mounting to a base makes the awning stronger but will give it more a stiff appearance. Other alternatives include mounting the paper awning to a wood or plastic frame or folding the paper back and forth to create a rippled affect.

- *Chimneys* – You can also use paper to create square or round chimneys. Because chimneys are relatively small even in larger scales, it's best to create the form by folding or rolling the paper. Determine the width of the chimney side and then multiply this by four for a rectangular chimney or by two for a round chimney. To complete the rectangular chimney, fold the paper in equal widths four times and glue the end together. You can also leave a little extra to create a fold for gluing. To create a round chimney, roll the paper and glue the ends together.

- *Downspouts and gutters* – If you look at real life structures you'll see several different types of downspouts and gutters. Many are u-shaped and can be created easily by folding a length of paper into three equal parts. For the most realistic affect mount two pieces of paper together before folding, making sure that both pieces are face up. This will ensure that the outside and the inside of the gutter has a finished look. You can also roll paper to create round downspouts, and attach multiple pieces together to form bends and directional changes.

- *Other roof details* – Roofs – especially commercial roofs – have several different detail parts. These details are subtle yet important way to distinguish a model building and make it appear more realistic. We've already discussed chimneys. You can use similar techniques to create step housings and air conditioning units. Many of these elements are relatively easy to create because they are rectangular structures. Often you can draw details onto the paper to finish off the shape. For example, use a black marker to draw in the vents and dials on air conditioning units.

The previous section reviewed the practices of setting interiors slightly back in a building to create depth. However, detailed interiors do not necessarily work for all structures, especially when the windows are smaller, have multiple panes or are higher up on the structure. Examples include residential houses and the upper windows of factories and warehouses. In this situation, the best strategy is often to make the windows appear open.

The mere presence of an open window automatically provides the illusion of depth, whether there is a detailed interior behind it. Most windows open in one of two ways: they lift up from the bottom or fold inward or outward from either the bottom or top. To create a window that's lifted up from the bottom, cut out the window panes and then re-glue the bottom pane partially behind the top pane (or leave it off completely).

Open and half-open windows are good way to add the illusion of depth.

To create a window that's tilted in or out, cut the pane on three sides and bend it inward or outward along the remaining edge. You can use the same strategy to create open doors – cut the door along three sides and then fold the door inward or outward. You may want to glue another copy of the window or door over top of the exposed area of the bend to create a more finished look.

If you want to avoid more cutting and folding – especially when it comes to small parts – you can always look for die cut objects to provide details for your scenes and structures. There are several companies that provide these kinds of details for model railroads but don't limit yourself to these sources. You can also find a lot of possibilities in the paper craft section of your nearest craft store.

Several companies make die cut objects for use in scrapbooking, specifically what is generally known as the decoupage style of scrapbooking. Manufacturers make a wide range of scaled-down everyday items to meet the needs of this style such as brackets, clocks, gears, metal signs, etc. Many of these objects even come with a weathered or worn look and they reflect a range of different historical time periods.

Ambitious modelers can even create their own die cuts. Several companies make die cutting machines designed for home use, priced at $200 to $300. You can purchase pre-designed artwork through cartridges and downloads or design your own elements from scratch using the machine's native software or a vector-based image editing program. You can also download vector-based images from the Internet and use the machine to cut them out.

Forced Perspective

Another effective strategy to add depth to paper models is forced perspective. Forced perspective employs an optical illusion to make certain objects or part of an object appear further away. Our brains use the size of an object in relation to other objects to determine the distance of that object from us. The smaller the object, the further it is from us. By purposely making an object or part of that object smaller we can fool the brain into thinking it's further away.

Amusement parks frequently use forced perspective to make buildings appear larger and higher. When constructed a two or three story building, the park purposely designs the upper floors to be smaller. One of the best examples is Cinderella's Castle in Disneyworld. The parapets on each level of the castle get smaller and smaller as you move to the top, making the castle look much higher. Other buildings in the park such as Belle's Castle are deliberately scaled even smaller to appear as though they're off in the distance.

These examples illustrate the two main forced perspective strategies that you can employ on your model railroad. You can compress your stories to make multi-story buildings look taller and you can make some buildings deliberately smaller to make them appear further back. Both strategies are best employed with objects that are at least somewhat set back from the front of the layout. They also tend to work best when there are other objects that can be viewed in relation to them.

Amusement parks almost always employ forced perspective beginning with the second story of a building. In the case of a model railroad you probably don't need to use this type of forced perspective until you get to at least the third or fourth floor. This is based on the angle of view. In an amusement park, you're standing on the ground looking up; with a model railroad you're generally looking straight on or even down.

Your use of distance based forced perspective depends largely on the overall depth of your layout. Almost any layout background should feature at least some objects or illustrations that are scaled down. For deeper layouts and certain types of scenes you'll want to employ this type of forced perspective from at least three-quarters away from the front of the layout. Urban scenes especially benefit from the placement of smaller than scale buildings on the fourth, third or even second street back.

One of the easiest methods of applying forced perspective is to move one scale down from your layout's actual scale. In other words, an O scale layout would feature background buildings in HO scale. An HO scale layout would use background buildings in N scale, etc. However, it's best to keep scales and ratios in mind when employing this method. Most forced perspective buildings use 75% as a general multiplier for successive levels or background. The next level up or back is 75% of the previous one.

HO scale is around 50% of the total size of O scale and N scale is around 55% of HO scale. That doesn't necessarily preclude them from this type of use, it simply means that you need to set them further back or upward to achieve the right perspective. The percentage of the original model or level should go down as you move further away from it.

This trick also works with smaller details. For example, you can use a smaller door to create the illusion that the door is set back in a vestibule or entrance way.

Keep in mind too that certain material patterns require a set scale while others are more flexible. For example, in most cases brick (and other man made materials) must be scale to look correctly in the context of the layout.

High-rail and Paper Scenery

Paper-based scenery and structures be as simple or complex as necessary to meet the needs of the specific model railroad. Using a full kit or some brick sheets and doors and windows you can create pretty-decent looking building that would be at home on almost any train layout. That model will look even better if you bump out a couple of features such as awnings, trim and signs and inset the windows and doors. It can look even better still if you use chalks to weather the brick to show general wear, water staining, etc. The point is that paper-based scenery is only limited by the amount of time and strategy you're willing to apply to it.

However, natural materials can often be used with multiple scales. Rock, stone and water don't necessarily have a set scale length and height. The only requirement is whether it looks good to you. This can even be true for metal patterns. In this case, it pays to experiment to get different effects.

Conversely, you may want to apply a "cut down" strategy regarding lengths and widths. This a technique often used on O scale modeling where the lengths of locomotives and freight cars are deliberately shortened. Most manufactured O scale buildings also use the "cut down" strategy. These buildings are often used in high-rail and prototype modeling environments.

Although the bricks, windows and doors may be scale, the overall building size is not. (Unless you're operating a fairly-small store or living in a pretty cramped house.) Even in a highly-detailed environment, cutting down lengths and widths is a practical strategy to produce scenery that looks good but doesn't take up an excessive amount of room.

Weathering

Railroaders have long employed the technique of weathering to give models an aged and more realistic appearance. This typically done with paint and powders. You can weather paper models as well. You just need to choose weathering materials that are more conducive to the material. The best tools for weathering paper structures are artist's chalks and markers.

You'll find most of the artist's chalks and markers you'll need at the craft supply store, in either the art section or the paper craft/scrapbook section. Simple sidewalk chalks and school markers are not subtle enough for this type of weathering. It's important to purchase the denser chalk designed for use in chalk drawings and the more flexible markers designed for use in creating cards and scrapbook pages.

Paper can be weathered using artist's chalk.

You'll want to experiment with different tones and colors, ideally on a piece of scrap paper or left over cut away first. Use a light hand to apply the color and use your finger or a fine brush to spread the color. Work in one small area at a time. Unlike weathering plastic, it's very difficult to remove weathering on paper once it's in place. However, you can cover up mistakes by applying another layer of paper.

Whether to weather before or after you construct a building depends on the type of base involved. For lighter bases such as no base or chipboard it's generally easier to weather your sheets before applying to the base and assembling the sides. For heavier bases such as foam board, wood or Styrofoam you can weather the building after it's constructed.

The amount of weather depends on the overall look and feel you'd like on your layout. Some people before a more gritty and industrial look while others like things fresh and clean. That's why I usually don't apply a lot of weathering to my designs in Scenery Sheets. I'd rather leave it up the modeler to choose their own vision rather than forcing them into using mine.

Take your inspiration from real life objects when deciding what to weather on paper models (just as you would on a plastic or metal model). Here are some potential weathering areas:

- Rust and other corrosion on buildings
- Chips, crack and fading on brick face
- Water stains on buildings and walls
- Moss and other growths on buildings and walls
- Graffiti on buildings and walls

PROJECTS OVERVIEW

The best way to learn about using paper-based scenery in model railroading is to dive into some projects. The second half of this book contains several practical projects that you can apply to any O scale, HO scale or N scale model train layout. Each project includes the following:

- Introduction to the project – an overview of the project and its application
- Tools and materials – a list of the tools and materials required to complete the project
- Tips and strategies – any insights about the project and ways to make it easier or better
- Step by step instructions – how to complete the project start to finish

Also included are the source paper sheets required to complete the project such as grass, brick, roads, etc. These papers are selections from the Scenery Sheets line of products. To use these sheets, fold open the page and carefully cut the entire page containing the sheet out of the book. Normally Scenery Sheets are printed to the edge of the paper.

Because of publishing and binding limitations, the sheets included in this book are not printed to the edge so you will need to do some trimming. They are also a much thinner paper. If you prefer to work with thicker sheets printed to the edge, visit scenerysheets.com to purchase a Project Kit to accompany the projects in the book. Our standard 80 lb. sheets are approximately the thickness of the cover of this book.

Depending on the type of project, there may be specific materials for each scale. For example, roads must be sized according to scale so the grade crossing project includes roads for O scale, HO scale and N scale. Other materials such as stone, metal and water are not necessarily scale specific – just cut the materials relative to your scale.

When working on these projects, don't forget to reference the information presented in the first part of the book – especially the tips and strategies included for cutting, folding and gluing. These are essential skills to master when producing paper scenery and models. If you have any questions about these projects, feel free to email me directly at dom@scenerysheets.com.

In addition to the photos in this book, more photos are available at scenerysheets.com – choose Project Photos from the menu at the top of the page. Also, throughout the photos in this book I've used a pen to mark lines and measurements. I did that to make sure the marks stood out in the photos. Normally, it's best to make all marks, lines and measurements in pencil so they can be easily erased.

6

Background Project #1

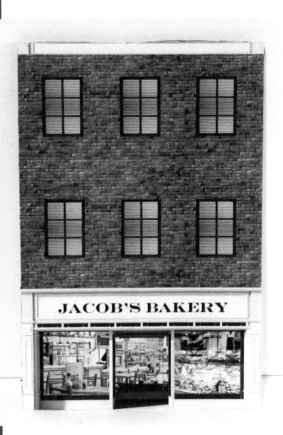

Flat Front Building

Create a background structure to add depth and interest on your model train layout.

INTRODUCTION

Flat front buildings are a great way to add depth to your train layout or fill in gaps where a three-dimensional building won't fit properly. Train layouts often run up against a wall or other structure such as a column. Covering walls and other structures with flat front building extends the scene and provides the illusion that the town or city continues beyond the layout. It's also an effective way to add more industries that can be serviced by your railroad.

In this project, you'll create a flat front building using the materials provided. To make things easier, the flat front building in this book is already complete with details such as doors and windows. This project provides an opportunity for you to practice basic techniques such as cutting, trimming and gluing onto a base.

TOOLS AND MATERIALS

Provided in this book:

- Flat front building

Required to complete the project:

- Cutting tool – scissors, hobby knife or paper-trimmer
- Adhesive – diluted white glue or spray adhesive
- Brush – paint brush, sponge or other tool to apply the glue
- Base – foam board or balsa wood
- Folding tool or roller to spread down the model
- Flat surface to work on

TIPS AND STRATEGIES

- When cutting square patterns and straight edges such as this project, a paper-trimmer is easier, quicker and more accurate
- Make sure the glue covers the entire surface of the model to insure the edges stay down
- Spray-adhesives work well for this type of flat model, but is messier and less forgiving than diluted white glue
- Although this project is presented as a flat model, you could a short length of roof at the top and extra length of brick on the sides to make this a partial building. You could also use thin strips of roof and brick to cover the top and side edges.

STEP BY STEP INSTRUCTIONS

Step 1: Use a cutting tool to cut around the edges of the model. Be sure to remove any stray threads or scraps of paper along the edges using the scissor edge technique described earlier in the book.

Step 2: Measure the size of the model and cut the base to fit the size of the model. Another option is to trace the model. If you do trace the model, make sure you cut on the inside edge of the line. Otherwise the base will come out slightly larger than the model.

Step 3: Flip the model over and use a paint brush or other applicator tool to cover the back with glue. Make sure you cover the entire surface evenly, spreading out any glops or bubbles of glue. If using a spray-adhesive, make sure you cover the entire surface with an even spray – you may need to over-spray to cover the corners.

Step 4: Flip the model back over and position it on the base. Carefully smooth down the model using your hands, folding tool or roller. Make sure there are no bubbles or wrinkles. If using a spray-adhesive, you'll likely only get one shot at positioning the model so flip slowly and deliberately.

Note: If the corners curl up a bit don't panic. Just apply a bit more glue at the corner and then smooth the corner back down. Use a damp cloth or slightly wet paper towel to remove any excess glue that squeezes out on the side.

Step 5: Use a black magic marker to color in the top and edges. You could also cover these edges with a thin strip of roof material and brick material.

PROJECT PHOTOS

Trim the edges off the model.

Measure and cut the base.

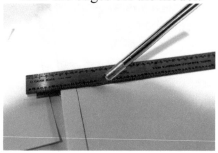

Use a straight edge to help with cuts.

Paint the rear side of the model with glue.

Press the model on the base.

Use black marker to color the edges.

Completed Model.

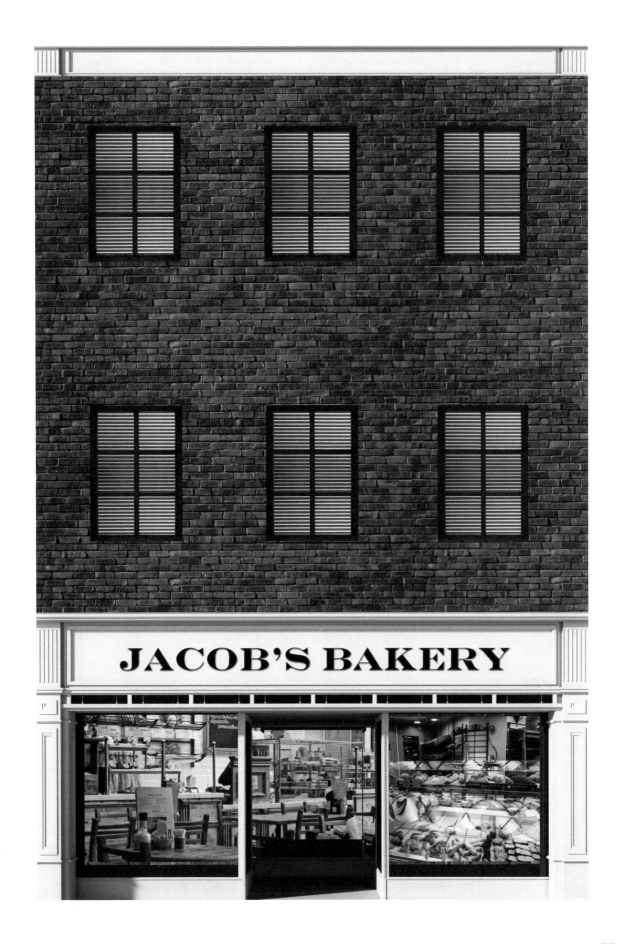

THIS PAGE INTENTIONALLY LEFT BLANK

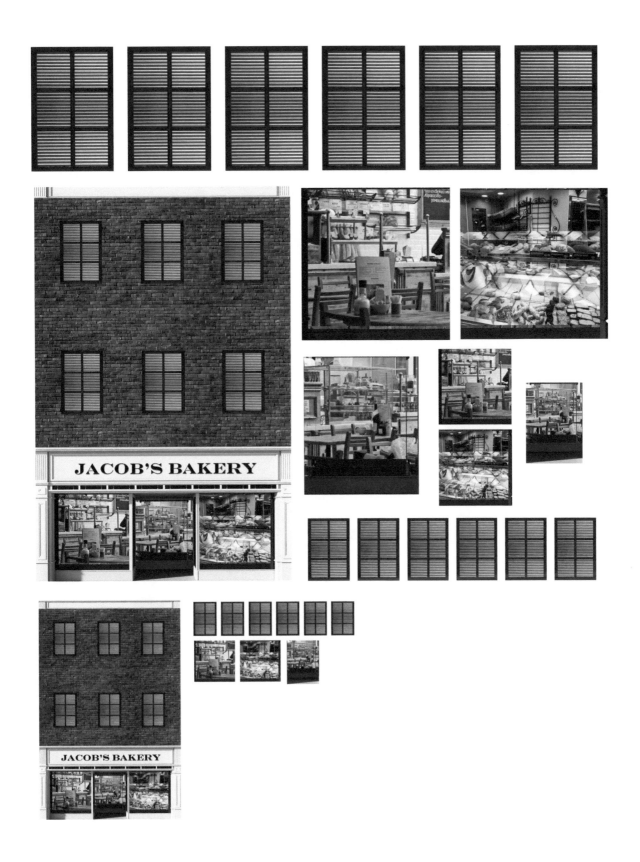

THIS PAGE INTENTIONALLY LEFT BLANK

7

Background Project #2

Retaining Wall and Portal

Create a stone retaining wall for use as a background on your layout or along an upper tier.

INTRODUCTION

Retaining walls are a common site along many rail lines and a long-time staple on model railroads. In addition to serving as backgrounds, retaining walls are also an extremely practical way to finish off an upper deck or tier on a train layout. They fit into just about any scene and allow you to maintain a straight edge along the side of the upper level. This takes up much less room than an embankment or sloping edge.

In this project, you'll create a stone retaining wall with bump-outs to create the illusion of depth. This project demonstrates the use of raised areas to create more depth and will give you a chance to practice cutting out a non-straight area (the portal and opening).

TOOLS AND MATERIALS

Provided in this book:

- Stone retaining wall
- Bump-out sections

Required to complete the project:

- Cutting tool – scissors, hobby knife or paper-trimmer
- Adhesive – diluted white glue or spray adhesive
- Brush – paint brush, sponge or other tool to apply the glue
- Base – foam board or balsa wood
- Folding tool or roller to spread down the model
- Flat surface to work on

TIPS AND STRATEGIES

- To create a more layered effect, you can cut the base stone wall into smaller strips, then mount the strips over lapping each other on the base – an extra sheet of stone wall is provided so that you can practice this technique in addition to building the model
- You can vary the size and spacing of the bump-outs to change the overall look of the retaining wall.
- Retaining walls often have water and/or rust stains running down them. You can create these types of stains by marking the stone paper with artist chalks.
- Use a straight edge such as a ruler when cutting up the base.
- Make sure all your folds are clean and crisp before applying glue.

STEP BY STEP INSTRUCTIONS

Step 1: Use a cutting tool to cut around the edges of the stone wall strips and bump outs to remove the border. You can also adjust the length and height of the stone strips to fit your layout. Be sure to remove any stray threads or scraps of paper along the edges using the scissor edge technique described earlier in the book.

Step 2: Measure the size of the stone strips and bump-outs and cut the base to fit the size of each. When measuring and cutting the base, make sure you make it slightly smaller than the size of your stone strips and bump-outs so that you can fold the excess over the edges to hide them. Just as in the previous project, you can modify the overall size of the bump-outs by extended the area of the sides and top – or simply fold over the excess to cover the edges.

Step 3: Pre-fold the overlap pieces over the base to get a clean, crisp crease in the paper prior to gluing. If necessary cut a slit between the sides and top of the overlap. Fold over the base once to mark the crease and then use a straight-edge to finish out the fold.

Step 4: Flip the first stone strip over and use a paint brush or other applicator tool to cover the back with glue. Make sure you cover the entire surface evenly, spreading out any glops or bubbles of glue. If using a spray-adhesive, make sure you cover the entire surface with an even spray – you may need to over-spray to cover the corners.

Step 5: Flip the stone strip back over and position it on the base. Carefully smooth down the model using your hands, folding tool or roller. Make sure there are no bubbles or wrinkles. If using a spray-adhesive, you'll likely only get one shot at positioning the model so flip slowly and deliberately.

Step 6: If you're keeping the stone strip flat, fold the extra sides and top over the edge of the base to hide it. If you're using flaps to create some depth, score the underside of the base and fold the base and the flaps down together. Glue the sides and top to each other to hold them firm

Step 7: Repeat steps 3-5 for each of the stone strips, then repeat them again to create the bump-outs.

Step 8: Mount the bump-outs on top of the strips.

PROJECT PHOTOS

Trim the edges off the model.

Measure the base factoring overlap.

Cut out the base pieces.

Create your folds.

Glue the paper to the base.

Fold over and glue the edges.

Make sure flaps are glued down.

Glue paper onto bump outs.

Glue on the bump outs.

Completed Model.

THIS PAGE INTENTIONALLY LEFT BLANK

THIS PAGE INTENTIONALLY LEFT BLANK

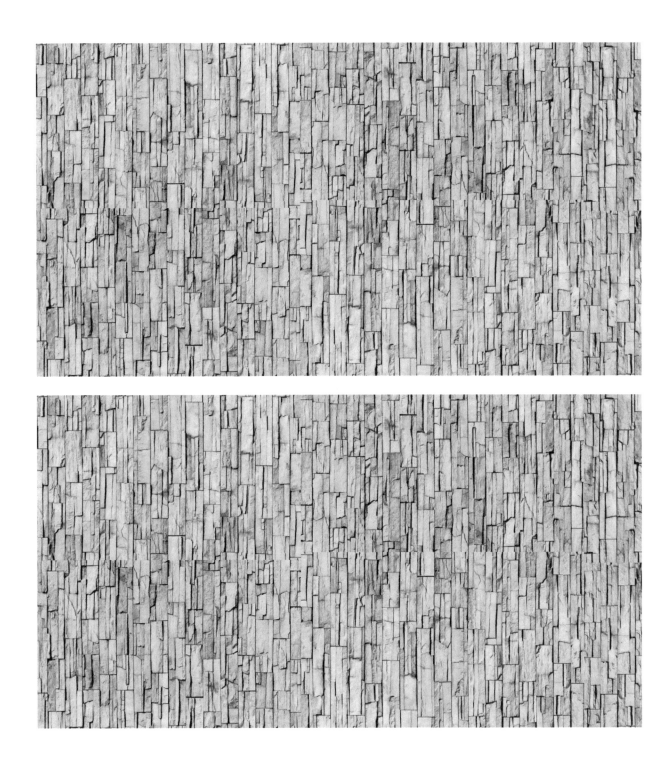

THIS PAGE INTENTIONALLY LEFT BLANK

8

Landscape Project #1

Railroad Grade Crossing

Transform a standard straight piece of Lionel Fastrack or MTH Realtrax into a realistic looking grade crossing.

INTRODUCTION

Most model railroads feature both rails and roads and it's likely that the roads will cross over the rails at some point. There are several off the shelf products available for most track types, however you can make an even better looking grade crossing with paper road sheets and some glue.

In this project, you'll use a pre-printed sheet to create a grade crossing on your choice of either a 10" straight of Lionel Fastrack or MTH Realtrax, including the road leading up to the track. You'll have the opportunity to practice the technique of saturating paper to mold against an angled base and cutting and placing smaller pieces.

TOOLS AND MATERIALS

Provided in this book:

- Railroad crossing road sheets
- Asphalt pieces for inside the rails

Required to complete the project:

- Cutting tool – scissors, hobby knife or paper-trimmer
- Adhesive – diluted white glue
- Brush – paint brush, sponge or other tool to apply the glue
- 10" straight piece of either Lionel Fastrack or MTH Realtrax

TIPS AND STRATEGIES

- Because this project involves saturating and molding the paper against the roadbed of the track, it's best to use a diluted white glue product as the adhesive. Diluted white glue works best for this type of technique.
- For this project, you may want to produce your own diluted white glue, using a higher resolution of water to glue – at least a 60:40 ratio.
- Take care to keep the pieces of the grade crossing below the top of the rails and leave a small gap in front of the rails to avoid affect the wheels of the trains.
- Although this project focuses on converting a combine track and roadbed product to a grade crossing, you can also use this strategy to create a grade crossing with track without embedded roadbed such as Lionel O or O27 or Atlas. To create a grade crossing with track without roadbed, mount the road paper on a base material such as foam board or balsa wood first.

STEP BY STEP INSTRUCTIONS

Note: This technique works best when used with track already in place on the train layout.

Step 1: Use a cutting tool to cut around the edges of the road and asphalt pieces to remove the border. Be sure to remove any stray threads or scraps of paper along the edges using the scissor edge technique described earlier in the book.

Step 2: Flip the first road piece over and use a paint brush or other applicator tool to cover the back with glue. Make sure you cover the entire surface evenly, spreading out any glops or bubbles of glue. Use enough glue that the road strip becomes soft and pliable.

Step 3: Flip the road strip back over and place it on top of the roadbed on one side of the track. Press it down firmly, molding it to the contours of the roadbed. Use your fingers to smooth out any bumps or wrinkles. If necessary, you can apply another coat of diluted white glue on top of the paper to make it more pliable.

Step 4: Repeat Step 3 with the other strip of road on the other side of the track.

Step 5: Flip the first asphalt piece over and use a paint brush or other applicator tool to cover the back with glue. Make sure you cover the entire surface evenly, spreading out any glops or bubbles of glue. Use enough glue that the road strip becomes soft and pliable.

Step 6: Flip the asphalt strip back over and place it in between two of the rails, in line with the road piece you previously glued onto the roadbed. Press it down firmly, molding it to the contours of the roadbed. Use your fingers to smooth out any bumps or wrinkles.

Step 7: Repeat Step 6 with the other asphalt piece between the other two rails, making sure it lines up with the other pieces.

PROJECT PHOTOS

Start with track mounted in place.

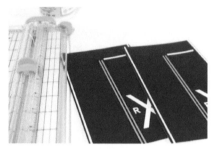
Trim the road pieces.

Cut the first road strip with glue.

Mold the road strip onto the roadbed.

Seal with diluted white glue if necessary.

Measure the width of the road.

Measure the space between the rails.

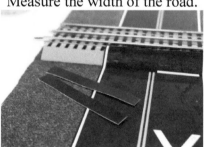
Cut and glue asphalt strips.

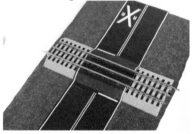
Completed Model.

THIS PAGE INTENTIONALLY LEFT BLANK

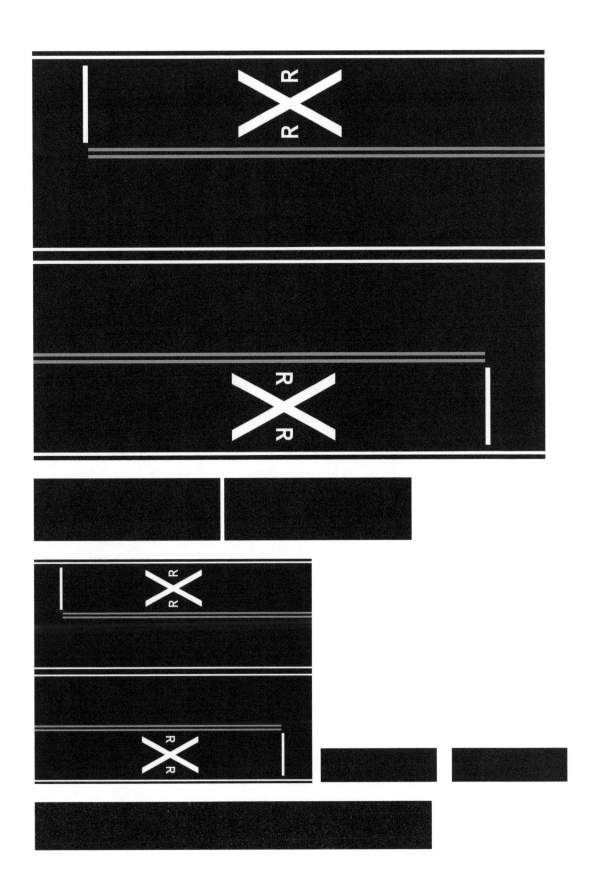

THIS PAGE INTENTIONALLY LEFT BLANK

9

Landscape Project #2

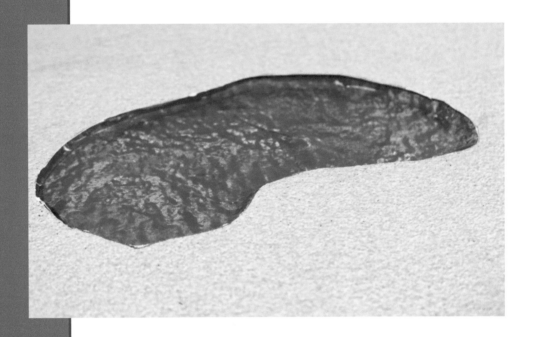

Fishing Pond

Create a small fishing pond on your train layout using paper printed with water and sand.

INTRODUCTION

Water features always make a nice scenic addition to a model train layout. Not all layouts have the room for a large lake or river, but most have a bit of space for a small fishing pond. In fact, a fishing pond or swimming hole can be an effective way to fill in an odd shaped gap that is too small to accommodate a structure.

In this project, you'll create a small pond by raising up an area of your layout and then carving out the area for the water. It gives you a chance to work with oddly shaped pieces and the technique of creating depth using paper scenery.

TOOLS AND MATERIALS

Provided in this book:

- Water sheet
- Sand sheet

Required to complete the project:

- Cutting tool – scissors or hobby knife
- Adhesive – diluted white glue
- Regular white glue or Modge Podge Dimensional Magic
- Brush – paint brush, sponge or other tool to apply the glue
- Base – foam board

TIPS AND STRATEGIES

- For most of these projects you can use either foam board or wood as a base. However, this project works best with foam board since it's easier to carve and layer.
- If you've used plywood or another hard material as the base for your train layout, it's best to build up the area around the pond as described in the steps below. However, if you have a foam or Styrofoam base on your layout you can skip the steps related to building up the area around the pond and carve out the area for the pond directly on your layout.
- This project creates the illusion of rippled water by applying a layer of glue on top of the paper once it's been applied to the base. You can create this affect using standard white glue but the Dimensional Magic product mentioned in the materials list will allow to create a more sculpted look.
- You can add boats, swimmers or fish into the glue on top of the paper before it dries.

STEP BY STEP INSTRUCTIONS

Step 1: Cut the shape of your pond out of the first piece of foam board. You can choose any shape you like, as long as it falls within the size of the water sheet.

Step 2: Place the foam board with the cut-out shape on top of the water sheet and use a pencil or blue pen to trace the shape on the water sheet.

Step 3: Use a hobby knife to cut out the shape – follow the traced line but stay about a quarter of an inch beyond it. The goal is to create a piece of water that is slightly larger than the cut-out of the foam board. This will allow you to fold it over to cover the inside edge of the cut-out. Be sure to remove any stray threads or scraps of paper along the edges using the scissor edge technique described earlier in the book.

Step 4: Place the foam board with the cut-out shape on top of the sand sheet and use a pencil or blue pen to trace the shape on the sand sheet.

Step 5: Use a hobby knife to cut out the shape from the sand sheet – in this case stay directly on the traced line to the edge of the sand will line up with the edge of the pond.

Step 6: Mount the piece of foam board with the cut-out on top of a solid piece of foam board using white glue or diluted white glue.

Step 7: Flip the water piece over and use a paint brush or other applicator tool to cover the back with glue. Make sure you cover the entire surface evenly, spreading out any glops or bubbles of glue. Use enough glue that the water piece becomes soft and pliable.

Step 8: Flip the water piece back over and place it on top of the cut-out foam board. Press it down firmly, molding it to the contours of the cut-out. Don't worry if the water overlaps the edges of the cut-out; the sand sheet will cover it. Use your fingers to smooth out any bumps or wrinkles. You can also allow the glue to dry and then trim off the excess edges.

Step 9: Flip the sand piece over and use a paint brush or other applicator tool to cover the back with glue. Make sure you cover the entire surface evenly, spreading out any glops or bubbles of glue.

Step 10: Flip the sand piece back over and place it on top of the cut-out foam board, lining it up with the cut-out. Press it down firmly and use your fingers to smooth out any bumps or wrinkles.

Optional: Fill the water area with Dimensional Magic or an artificial water product. Use a toothpick or other small tool or even your finger to create ripples in the glue. This creates the allusion of movement once the glue is dry. You can also wait until the glue is partially hardened to add more ripples.

PROJECT PHOTOS

Cut your pond shape out of the base.

Trace the shape of the pond.

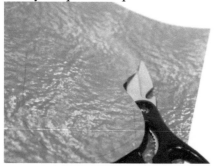

Cut the paper wider than the line.

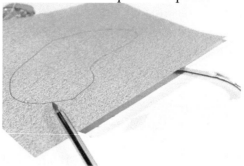

Trace the shape on the sand sheet.

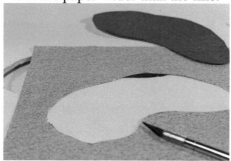

Cut the sand on the traced line.

Glue the water down over the base.

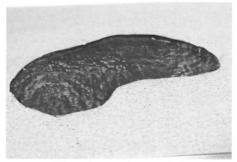

Glue down the model.

THIS PAGE INTENTIONALLY LEFT BLANK

THIS PAGE INTENTIONALLY LEFT BLANK

10

Structure Project

Bait & Tackle

Create a three-dimensional local fishing tackle store from a pre-printed pattern to go with your fishing pond.

INTRODUCTION

A well-designed model railroad includes a mix of structures of various shapes and sizes. Often, it's the small buildings that can make a scene. Barracuda's Bait & Tackle is a small local store conveniently located by the edge of a local fishing hole. The shop is the typical clapboard and metal structure you'd expect to find in this type of situation.

For this project, you'll construct a small three-dimensional building that's been fully pre-printed with windows, doors and other details. It's opportunity to take your cutting and gluing skills to the next level. Working with smaller structures first is a good way to get ready for dealing with larger, more custom builds.

TOOLS AND MATERIALS

Provided in this book:

- Bait and tackle front and side panel, rear panel and roof panel
- Extra signs and window inserts

Required to complete the project:

- Cutting tool – scissors or hobby knife
- Adhesive – diluted white glue or spray adhesive
- Brush – paint brush, sponge or other tool to apply the glue
- Base – foam board or balsa wood

TIPS AND STRATEGIES

- It's always a good idea to review all the instructions before beginning a model but this is especially true when constructing a three-dimensional model.
- As mentioned earlier in this book, a strategy for adding depth to a model is to cut out the windows and then place them underneath the main part of the model. This gives them a look that makes them appear to be inset.
- When mounting the extra signs included, you can add them directly to the model or mount them to a base and then mount that to the model.
- Although this model is already designed to be small and fit in a small space, you can make the model smaller by cutting down the sides to make the building shallower.
- To provide additional depth to the roof, fold it several times before mounting on the top of the model. This will give the metal print a corrugated look.

STEP BY STEP INSTRUCTIONS

Step 1: Cut all the pieces of the building off the pages to remove the white borders around them. Be sure to remove any stray threads or scraps of paper along the edges using the scissor edge technique described earlier in the book.

Step 2: Place the pieces on top of the foam board or balsa wood base and trace around the outside of the pieces. You don't need to cut to cover the flaps on the rear side of the building – just the printed area.

Step 3: Use a hobby knife or other cutting tool to cut the base pieces along the lines you created by tracing the model pieces.

Step 4: Line the model pieces up against the base pieces and mark the fold lines on the front of the building. Use these marks to cut the base to separate the front and sides of the building.

Step 5: Fold the sides of the model back using the folding techniques described earlier in this book. Make sure your folds are clean, even and crisp. Remember that good folds are the key to building good paper models.

Step 6: Flip the front and sides of the model over and use a paint brush or other applicator tool to cover only the front are with glue - do not apply glue to the sides now, only the front.

Step 7: Flip the front of the model back over and press it onto the corresponding base piece. Press it down firmly and use a folding tool or your fingers to smooth out any bumps or wrinkles.

Step 8: Line the sides up behind the folds and make any necessary adjustments – you may need to trim off some excess from the base. Use glue stick to connect the base sides to the front.

Step 8: Fold back the flaps on the rear side of the model. Make any final adjustments to the size or shape of the base piece for the back.

Step 9: Flip the rear side of the model over and use a paint brush or other applicator tool to cover just the back with glue (not the flaps) and press the rear side of the model onto the base.

Step 9: Paint the flaps with glue and attach them to the sides of the model. Paint each side with glue and attach them to the base. The side pieces will also cover the flaps from the back of the model. Make sure to smooth out any bumps or wrinkles.

Step 11: Carefully apply a thin line of glue along the top edge of the front, back and sides of the model. Place the roof of the model on top, resting on the glued top edges.

Optional: Mount of the extra signs to the base and glue it onto the front of the building.

PROJECT PHOTOS

Trim the edges off the model pieces.

Measure and cut the base pieces.

You don't need to mount the tabs.

Account for fold lines when cutting.

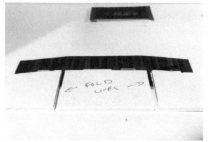

Check placement of base pieces.

Make the folds on the model.

Use a straight edge to get good folds.

Apply glue to front side.

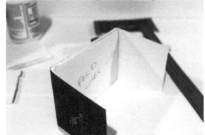

Attach front side to base.

Trim base if necessary.

88

PROJECT PHOTOS

Glue the sides to the base.

Glue the rear side to the base.

Glue the tabs down on the base sides.

Glue the sides over the tabs and base.

Glue the roof onto the model.

Cut out the sign.

Trace and cut out the base.

Color the edges of the base.

Glue sign onto base and onto building.

SCENERY SHEETS

EASY AND AFFORDABLE STRUCTURES, LANDSCAPES AND BACKGROUNDS FOR YOUR MODEL TRAIN LAYOUT.

Scenery Sheets features professional full color printing with four color processing, shadows and highlights to provide the illusion of depth, realistic images composited from real life photos and the ability to tile multiple sheets end to end and top to bottom to create a seamless scene.

Scenery Sheets are available in two sizes: 8.5"x11" and 13"x19" – both with full bleed printing to the edge. All patterns are available in O, HO, S, N and Z scales.

Scenery Sheets are designed to provide a full system for landscaping and adding structures to your layout – start with a kit or build from scratch. **There are over 200 Scenery Sheets available in several categories: Brick, Grass, Marble, Metal, Road, Rock, Roof, Sand, Stone, Water, Building kits, Backgrounds and more.**

Buy direct at scenerysheets.com and enter code SAVE20 to save 20% off orders of $20 or more. Shipping is always free. Be sure to check out rewards program to save even more on future purchases.

www.scenerysheets.com

Follow us on Facebook and Pinterest

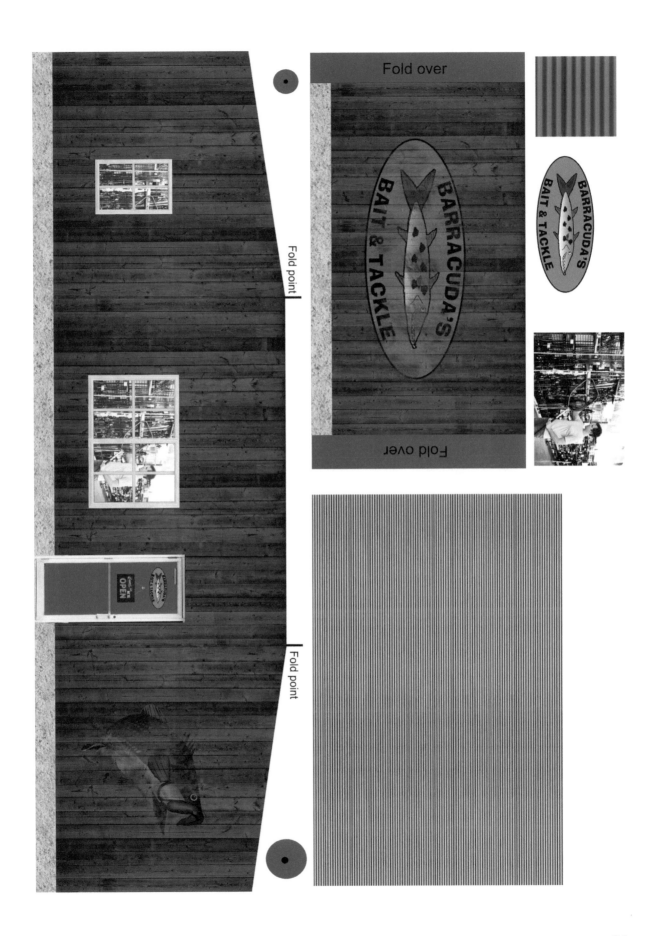

Fold over

Fold point

BARRACUDA'S BAIT & TACKLE

Fold over

Fold point

OPEN

THIS PAGE INTENTIONALLY LEFT BLANK

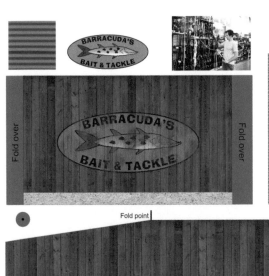

Fold over

Fold over

Fold point

Fold point

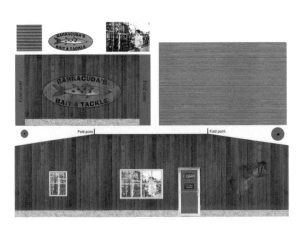

Fold over

Fold over

Fold point

Fold point

Other books by Dominic Villari:

Children's Books:

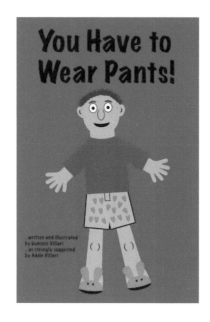

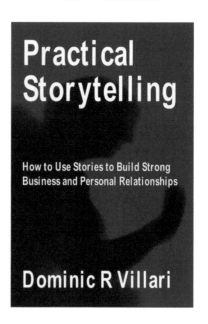

Fiction: Non-Fiction:

Visit www.figmentpress.com for more information.